To Hang Out the Washing

Joe Lake

Freshwater Publishing
an imprint of IP (Interactive Publications Pty Ltd)
Treetop Studio • 9 Kuhler Court
Carindale, Queensland, Australia 4152
sales@ipoz.biz
http://ipoz.biz/

© 2023, Joe Lake (text) and IP (design)
eBook versions © 2023

An earlier version of *To Hang Out The Washing* was published in time for Joe Lake's 92nd birthday on December 3rd 2017. The final edition became available for commercial release in 2023.

All rights reserved. Without limiting the rights under copyright reserved above, no part of this publication may be reproduced, stored in or introduced into a retrieval system, or transmitted, in any form or by any means (electronic, mechanical, photocopying, recording or otherwise), without the prior written permission of the copyright owner and the publisher of this book.

Printed in 12 pt Book Antiqua on 14 pt Avenir Book.

ISBN: 9781922830197 (PB); 9781876819897 (eBk)

 A catalogue record for this book is available from the National Library of Australia

To my mother Leah, in loving memory.

Acknowledgements

Commissioning Editor:
Kelly Hawke
Freshwater Productions

Editors:
Nada Morgan, Trish Lake
Freshwater Productions

Cover Design:
Jennifer Hillhouse

Book Design:
Dr David Reiter
Interactive Publications

Freshwater Productions wishes to thank Joe Lake's family, John, Anne, Daniel and Nikki; Trish, Ben, Jack, Kelly and Anna, and honour Joe's late wife and son, Bunty and Peter.

Thanks also to Prue Miller and Bill Morgan.

Contents

Acknowledgements	iv
Foreword	viii
Chapter One: 1940, a Second War for Dad, a Second Husband Missing for Mum	1
Chapter Two: Preparations for War	7
Chapter Three: Enlistment Day	21
Chapter Four: A Surprise Visitor in Khaki	46
Chapter Five: Luftwaffe Night Moves	65
Chapter Six: Tragedy Awaits	87
Chapter Seven: For Eddie, a Last Parade	98
Chapter Eight: From Teen Soldier to Sniper	111
Chapter Nine: And Into Germany	145
Chapter Ten: New Horizons and Final Respects	160

The author, Joe Lake (right) his brother, John (left), and another worker (centre) at the Warragamba Dam construction site, New South Wales, around 1948.

Joe's older brother John Henry Lake who was a pilot in the RAF, in uniform in England in August 1943.

Joe Lake at Point Lookout, holding his mother Leah's picture, photographed for The Australian War Memorial's 'Reflections' project.

Image courtesy of Melissa Anderson

Foreword

Some twenty years ago, stretched out on the veranda of my home that overlooks Cylinder Beach on North Stradbroke Island, I had the pleasure of a visit from Jack, one of my grandsons. The near perfect weather that afternoon was being complemented by a light northerly sea breeze that was starting to make its presence felt, typical of the pleasant days we take for granted here in this part of Queensland, Australia.

Jack, who was then a teenager, had already travelled widely from an early age with his journalist parents who were working around the world, mainly London and Washington, where he reckoned he'd spent some of his happier school days. It would be fair to say that Jack's a very pleasant boy, not bad looking, and maybe a little shy or modest. All in all, he'd got quite a lot to be thankful for, and not just his globetrotting.

When I asked Jack his age, he told me that, only a few weeks before, his fifteenth birthday had been the fulfilment of a great year in his life. He'd finally been in one place long enough to appreciate the friendship of schoolmates, giving him an opportunity to participate in team sports again, besides being able to get back into sailing, surfing, and tennis. 'Really, Poppa,' he told me, 'you've no idea how exciting life can be for the likes of my generation. At your age it would be hard for you to understand.' And then with a grin, 'Do you think you could still remember what you were doing when you were my age, Poppa? What would a similar year have been like in your day?'

Casting my mind back, I realised my fourteenth year would have been spent mainly during 1940, and while I was still trying to unwind my past, there was a call on Jack's mobile.

'Sorry, Poppa, I've got to go. It's a friend over on Main Beach. He's pretty sure there's a wave starting to build up and reckons I'd be silly to miss it.'

Jack was obviously eager to get over there. He smiled apologetically and asked, 'Do you think maybe you could tell me about your earlier years some other time?' Then suddenly he was gone.

I looked over the balcony just in time to see him taking off in haste, his much dented but very prized surfboard fixed firmly under his arm.

Jack was all too aware I'd been steering a little clear of the "fast lane" for quite some time — taking regular afternoon siestas, seldom going in the surf, always leaving parties before midnight and that sort of thing, provoking me into thinking perhaps it might be of interest to him that I hadn't always lived like that, and that years ago I'd had my highs and lows just like him.

As I tried to slip into my afternoon nap, I found my thoughts turning to the events of 1940. Although over sixty years had elapsed and, even though my thoughts had seldom ventured into that particular era for many years, strange though it may seem, I could still recall that time in my life as though it was only yesterday. It wasn't a case of being able to remember 1940 – for me, my fourteenth year was a year that I was never able to forget, prompting me to jot it down, if only to give Jack a basis for comparison.

My daughter, Patricia, eager to see me involved in something different, thought it was a great idea and gave me the use of an old laptop.

After tapping out the first couple of pages I found it wasn't going to be the chore I'd imagined it would be. Though I'd never used a keyboard before, this story wasn't just being written, it was being re-enacted in my mind as it was put to print. Apart from that, it gave me the opportunity to let Jack know, his fourteenth year however entertaining it had been for him, he certainly did not hold a monopoly on excitement.

As I kept tapping away, it became clear that there would be too many loose threads left hanging if I cut the story short at 1941. I therefore "fast-forwarded", through the middle war years to give an insight into some of my experiences in Europe, before and after D-Day. I'd found it a little sad, but not too hard, to bid a final farewell to a lifestyle within the environs of the many tall smoke stacks and picturesque canals that symbolised the English midlands, before looking further afield and eventually becoming captivated, completely lost in the tranquillity of a subtropical island.

The reader should be warned that while there is no question as to the authenticity of this story, some minor incidents may be slightly out of sequence, some names may have been incorrectly spelt and others have been changed where necessary to protect personal reputations. If any errors have been made, it would be as a result of some eighty years' time lapse, and since it has been written entirely from memory, there is always a possibility that some minor detail may have been unintentionally omitted.

***

This is an authentic account from the world war that broke out during September, 1939, as seen through the eyes of a fourteen-year-old Birmingham boy – my eyes – more than eighty years ago, the scene set during 1940, early in the second year of the second inglorious "World War".

The first six months of the war had produced little fighting, as each side cautiously sounded out common borders, sea-lanes and airspace. Then, without any fanfare, early in the second week of April, 1940, the Germans took the initiative, invading Denmark and Norway, ending months of speculation as to when the so-called "Phoney War" would end and the real confrontation would begin. These actions made it clear to the rest of the world that Hitler's Germany held little respect for the neutralities of other countries, and had not the slightest consideration for the lives of innocent civilians.

During the second week in May, with little or no warning, the city of Rotterdam was bombed, along with other cities in Holland and Belgium. Parts of Western Europe were being introduced to Blitzkrieg. The powerful Luftwaffe also began attacking British and French forces deployed along the French-German border, paving the way for Germany's ultramodern army to make swift armoured thrusts into Belgium and France.

The situation grew progressively worse for the Allies after the Belgian Government had been forced into capitulation, the loss of the small Belgian Army strategically weakening part of the British-held sector of the Western Front. But more significantly, a bigger impact of the surrender was the way in which the British Expeditionary Force had suddenly been shown up for what it really was; a stop-gap force of willing men, the majority of whom were ill-equipped and ill-trained, with little or no knowledge of modern warfare.

There were similarities with this British Expeditionary Force and the one of their fathers, who struggled through Flanders a couple of decades before. Adding to the nostalgia, they'd been rigged out with mostly the same obsolete weapons and occupied much of the same sections of the line. During those early weeks of spring 1940, the strains of "It's a Long Way to Tipperary" were being heard again like ghostly voices from the past, echoing the untold miseries and torment of that "War to end all Wars" across the otherwise picturesque, green, rolling hills and poppy-bearing meadows of northwest France.

Makeshift training programs for British infantry recruits in the autumn of 1939 were equivalent to little more than a couple of months romping on Salisbury Plain, possibly to see how they'd cope with heavy army boots together with their sudden departure from the quieter, easy-going comforts of civilian life. The only other requirement must have been to ensure their metabolism wouldn't reject a more than regular intake of bully beef along with plenty of other hard tack.

As in 1916 during the Battle of the Somme, it was sheer numbers the War Department was seeking; there just wasn't enough time for proper training. Many of these unfortunate soldiers to-be also suffered the unenviable position of being led by peacetime officers of questionable suitability for war service. Most officers were proficient, many of them brilliant, but there were a few high-ranking regular officers who, after spending so many years on the Indian sub-continent had inadvertently acquired a tinge of the Raj, the very ordinary performances of some, suggesting nepotism may have been instrumental in their rise to higher echelons.

Ground to air co-operation that existed between the Army and the Royal Air Force in 1940 had been little better than what their fathers had experienced during the infancy days of the Royal Flying Corps on the Western Front, almost twenty-five years earlier. By contrast, the Luftwaffe's collaboration with the Wehrmacht when carrying out their many lightning attacks in the spring of 1940 introduced new dimensions to warfare, these yet to be listed in the annals of the British Army.

By the middle of May, the British Expeditionary Force (BEF) along with its French ally, were driven into all-out retreat from positions they'd held along the German border, most of the British moving westward towards the coast. This untimely withdrawal brought about many acts of heroism on the part of some British units, even though their ranks had been stacked with young Territorial soldiers, many of whom until recent months had only donned khaki on weekends. In this hopeless situation, they were repeatedly called upon to fight rearguard actions against a ruthless enemy, one that was highly trained and unquestionably the most technically advanced fighting force the world had ever known.

Not surprisingly, towards the end of May, this one-sided campaign was approaching its foregone conclusion, the bulk of the British, along with some Allied forces, withdrawing to the beaches around the French port of Dunkirk. There, during the final days of May and the beginning of June, 1940, a massive sea-borne evacuation to England continued under round-the-clock bombing and shelling. The last survivors from the BEF were recuperating back in England by the 4th of June, and, from that day, it could be said, the task of defending democracy was now placed entirely in the hands of Britain and the British Commonwealth.

Back in Britain, there was a cautiously quiet "what

happens now attitude?" as the shocked population awaited the storm. On their return to Blighty, Dunkirk survivors, although still able to give the occasional thumbs-up or display a weary smile of relief for cameramen, portrayed a pitiful sight as they lined the docks and quays around the south-east coast of England. Many who'd suffered weeks of endless one-sided combat were still defiantly clasping a rifle, others got back with little more than their grimy tattered khaki and were barely identifiable as soldiers except that however disillusioned they may have been, held strong determinations to continue the conflict another day.

The army's unexpected return from France had brought with it a strange silence that spread over the length of Britain. 'Why?' was the question being asked.

Only yesterday it seemed the lassie from Lancashire, Gracie Fields, had "Wished them luck as she'd waved them goodbye", while the forces' sweetheart, Vera Lynn, had sincerely promised, "We'll Meet Again". But even the lovely Vera must have considered the army's early and somewhat un-orderly return from the Continent a little inauspicious.

Many heads in Whitehall had rolled or were awaiting the chop. One of them was none other than Birmingham's own Neville Chamberlain, who'd not been a well man, and was much too much the gentleman to have had to deal with the likes of Hitler and Ribbentrop. He'd graciously stepped down and was replaced as Prime Minister with Winston Churchill taking up leadership of a coalition government just weeks before on May 10.

Meanwhile, a couple of thousand miles away on the quieter side of the Atlantic there still existed a place where city lights continued to shine, a place where moviegoers were witnessing the emergence of a new teenage idol – Judy Garland, a songster from Minnesota. The young American had recently experienced a mythical dream that took her "Somewhere over the Rainbow". She'd soared way up high above chimney tops into a utopian land where only bluebirds fly, leaving all the dark clouds far behind. But here in Britain there weren't any such rainbows, or bluebirds – only dark clouds. Ones that masked the unexpected departure of Neville Chamberlain from office, others that shrouded the axing of one of the army's most popular and current top marching songs – "We're Gonna Hang out the Washing on the Siegfried Line". "Hang out the Washing" had been unofficially, but never-the-less, conveniently brushed under the carpet and stealthily removed from the repertoires of dance orchestras and music halls, and it was during those remorseful days of early summer 1940 that the British had begun to demonstrate their gift of being able to laugh at misfortunes. Following the army's untimely evacuation from the Continent, the song's heroic lyrics had become nothing less than nonsensical, but surprisingly the tune remained as popular as ever. "Hang out the Washing" was in fact still being sung amidst much laughter in pubs across the country, almost as if it had suddenly become the nation's adopted symbol of defiance, albeit patriotically performed at its loudest about half an hour before the towels went on.

While the British awaited the Germans' next move, they were slowly entering one of the darkest chapters in their history. The dire situation in which they found themselves during the late spring of 1940 was a direct result of Whitehall's penny-pinching and lack of foresight. While every bit as naive, the failure of the USA during the mid-thirties, permitting the excessive build-up of Germany's armed forces, and, worse, allowing Hitler's new army of Nazi thugs to march triumphantly into the Rhineland, could be said, was in effect, the day the Second World War really began. America, along with Britain and France, had failed to monitor and enforce the conditions of the Versailles Treaty, the harsh terms of which had been set down and rigorously demanded, in particular by President Wilson. That failure meant that tens of thousands of young teenagers like me, either by conscience or perhaps just wanting to exchange humdrum for a little excitement, were unofficially about to go to war.

On the Continent, the victorious Germans were rejoicing over the extraordinary achievements of their beloved Fatherland. Musicians of the Paris Conservatoire National were already busy rehearsing in readiness for an anticipated revival of Beethoven, Mahler and Wagner. Within days, soldiers of the Wehrmacht were celebrating along the banks of the Seine, intent on enjoying everything that Paris had to offer. The German High Command and its self-proclaimed military genius, ex-Corporal Adolf Schicklgruber, the fifty-year-old Bohemian megalomaniac, had in just a few weeks become the toast of the Third Reich. Fortunately, his early claims to fame in June, 1940, were to be overshadowed by his sole and ignorantly-applied control of the highly-trained and ultra-obedient German armed forces, his misguided and egotistically motivated directives ultimately resulting in a series of military defeats that culminated with the total devastating collapse of all Nazi resistance in Europe by early May, 1945.

Sadly, war clouds were soon to cast their ugly shadows over another European city; one that was considered to be as far away from Paris in miles as it was in elegancy and flair, except of course through the eyes of those who resided there. That city was my home, Birmingham, the heart of Britain, where this personal war account begins.

Chapter One: 1940, a Second War for Dad, a Second Husband Missing for Mum

Moving through the southern suburbs of Birmingham on the morning of June 3, 1940, a bus bound for the city was making slow progress, its overworked conductor repeatedly having to advise there was no more room upstairs and standing room only inside! There were signs of a little uneasiness among some passengers, after having heard a warning that air raids on England were likely to begin soon after the fall of Dunkirk. News agencies were indirectly advising that, as soon as Luftwaffe pilots ran out of targets on the Continent, their attention was expected to switch quickly to Britain's industrial cities, with Birmingham and Coventry almost certainly to be in the forefront.

The bus continued its way along the busy Stratford Road through the Midland city's inner suburbs, with most passengers endeavouring to display the usual stiff upper-lip. The shocking news of the complete collapse of all Allied resistance in France was slowly beginning to get through to the public. The conversations on the bus were that we might be about to experience our first air raid that morning, causing just a little concern to be evident on the faces of a few passengers. This was a trip that, for some reason, always seemed to take a bit longer on Mondays. I was on my way to work, after a weekend that had slipped by all too quickly.

The day before, I'd spent with my mother and brothers while anxiously awaiting news of my father, who was a soldier serving with the British Expeditionary Force in France. Dad was no stranger to France, certainly not the part that had been the scene of four years of bloody conflict in the First World War. Though I was just a thirteen-year-old when he re-enlisted two days after war broke out in September, 1939, his departure for the Continent only weeks later remains a vivid memory. Dad and his comrades, members of the Royal Warwickshire Regiment, seemed to be under the impression that the war would be over in a matter of months. He may have been trying to dispel our fears when he'd told Mum and my brothers of his plans to grow backyard mushrooms in our recently erected Anderson air raid shelter, just as soon as he got back home. We wondered if this was Dad's way of telling us that he thought it unlikely the shelter would ever be used for its intended purpose.

When the 31A council bus eventually pulled up outside Grey's store in Bull Street, near the centre of Birmingham, it left about three or four hundred yards for me to walk to Webley and Scott, Gunsmiths, where I'd been employed since leaving school a couple of months earlier. A future in engineering had been mapped out for me by my parents, and I began by receiving practical experience in the toolroom of this long-established firm that specialised in the manufacture of all kinds of equipment for military and sporting use.

Although the firm had retained its identity as one of the world's leading manufacturers of small arms, during the late 1930s Webley diversified in line with Government policy to match the arms build-up in Germany, mainly the growth of the Luftwaffe. Many of Webley's machine shops had subsequently been tooled up to produce components for Rolls-Royce aero-engines, including the Merlin that powered the Spitfire.

On the evening of Friday, June 7, I arrived home from work around a quarter past six as usual, to find my mother with her ear jammed hard against the radio, listening to the BBC news. The situation was grave. Even though it had been almost a week since the last survivors had been rescued from the beaches around Dunkirk, Mum had heard nothing that could throw more light on my father's whereabouts.

There was one small ray of hope. Our neighbours had heard there'd been soldiers at the local pub the night before and there was a strong possibility some may have been members of our own county regiment, the Warwicks.

After tea, my mother thought I should take a stroll to the Gospel Oak to see what I could find out, telling me that any bit of information might help explain Dad's absence. By the time I eventually arrived at the pub it was nearly nine o'clock and I was surprised to find the big crowd that crammed the public bar was already getting into singing mode. Their carryings-on made it hard for me to believe that only a couple of days earlier, the humbled British Army had suffered its biggest set-back in over two hundred years. Hardly the time for celebrations, I thought.

The army was well represented. Many of the soldiers frequenting the pub during the past nine months were serving with one of the locally-based heavy anti-aircraft batteries. This particular territorial unit of two or three hundred men, along with their guns, were encamped near the Robin Hood Golf Course, just a few hundred yards away, close enough for many of the gunners to have made the Gospel their second home. In the months ahead, these young artillerymen would be spending less time at the bar, and more time around their guns, much to the dismay of those unfortunate enough to be living within a mile of them.

Too young to enter the pub, I tried to make myself comfortable sitting on a concrete step near the entrance to the public bar, as I listened to a fine rendition of "Roses of Picardy", followed by a pretty loud but very ordinary version of "Lily of Laguna". I began to wonder if my little excursion was going to help in any way to resolve the mystery surrounding my father's whereabouts. The light was beginning to wane, but there was no let-up in the singing.

Suddenly a khaki-clad figure came shuffling backwards through swinging doors, almost falling on top of me. This fellow appeared to be very much under the weather, but since the forage cap screwed up beneath a shoulder epaulette bore the badge of the Royal Warwickshire Regiment, I thought I'd better try to have a natter with him.

'My father's in the same regiment as you,' I said, eventually able to get through to him. 'Is there any chance you'd know him?'

'Yeah, what's that you say, wass your name then?' he drawled, sounding like he'd been in the pub since the doors opened.

'I'm Joe Lake,' I told him. 'You see, my Dad was over in France and my mother would like to know why he hasn't returned along with other members of the regiment.'

'Well, I'm sorry to hear that son. And look, I don't know your father. But if he was over the other side with our mob, there are a couple of fellows down the other end of the bar who might know your dad.

'You just hang around here for half a mo' and I'll see if I can find someone to help you.'

But it was more than a few anxious moments of waiting and I began to feel his drinking had got the better of him and he'd forgotten me. The day had been a long one and I was just about to walk home. Then, while the revellers were well into harmonising a very touching and slightly sentimental version of "Smile Awhile", a song that, because of the woeful events of the past two or three weeks, could well have had some of the elderly reaching for their hankies, the soldier re-appeared. There were two others with him, one of them a warrant officer who looked more my father's age, and also showing more than just a little effect of a long evening session.

'So, you must be one of Sergeant Lake's lads,' said the sergeant major. 'And I hear he's not home yet. Is that right?'

'That's right, I'm Joe,' I told him 'and I'm here for my mother. She's very concerned to find out what's happened to him.'

'Your Dad's been a mate of mine for years,' the sergeant major told me.

'The last time I saw him was three or four weeks ago. We'd been hurriedly evacuating positions the battalion had held for several months, before moving off towards the coast.' He paused for a couple of seconds as though deep in thought; his right hand brushed slovenly across his forehead. Then with a kind of cheeky half-hearted smile he continued.

'The Jerries advanced quickly after a couple of surprise

Stuka attacks left us with a number of serious casualties besides severely depleting our artillery support. We'd had to move off in a hurry, leaving behind half of our medics to look after the worst of the wounded.'

Then, pausing again, he looked back towards his drinking companion, as if inviting him to confirm or add to what he'd told me. His mate appeared to vaguely nod his head in agreement but offered no comment and the sergeant major continued. He told me my father had also been temporarily left behind, explaining that Dad had been given the trusty task of destroying everything they weren't able to take with them. He'd stayed behind with a platoon of about twenty-five men. And, according to the sergeant major, it would have taken Dad about two hours to complete his assignment, ensuring nothing of any value to the enemy was left intact, before joining the huge column of men and equipment moving west along a road in the general direction of Dunkirk.

The camp they were to put to the torch contained a number of un-roadworthy vehicles, along with all of HQ Company's workshops as well as some stores and ammunition. There was also a well-stocked canteen and this was believed to have contained a considerable amount of liquor.

'Knowing your Dad as I do, I'm sure he would have used this opportunity to reward his platoon for their efforts and this could have easily resulted in their task taking more than two hours.

'If that was the case,' the sergeant major continued, 'and they'd left much later, there was a possibility he may not have been able to make use of the road that most of the Brigade moved off on. Your Dad may have been forced to head off in a more southerly direction.

'Look, Joe, I'm sure he'll be all right. I know your father well enough. He would have had everything under control. Now you go home and tell your Mum what I've told you.'

With that he gave me a pat on the back, and as I'd turned, they began making their way back into the pub. It was well after eleven o'clock by the time I began the walk home, my interest occupied by the many searchlights that were probing among well-dispersed clouds drifting northeast. Short summer nights had restricted training time for searchlight units and the worsening situation had now increased their importance to our defence. The searchlight activity was an unpleasant reminder that, although the fighting on the Continent might now be over, the war would go on. But for us, the stakes were now going to be so much higher.

The walk home gave me plenty of time to think about my father's plight, but I was unable to come up with a tactful way of explaining this likely, though somewhat questionable, situation to my mother. When the BBC had reported that between three and four hundred thousand British and Allied servicemen had been dramatically rescued from the beaches around Dunkirk, we all knew Mum had been expecting to see Dad home on leave or at least to have got word from him. Those news reports had come several days before and ever since she'd been preparing for his homecoming. I can still remember how painful it was for me to have to tell her that there was even the possibility that Dad may not have made it back to England.

The story his army mates had given me did nothing to ease my mother's despair. Her thoughts no doubt, would have gone back to a day twenty-four years earlier, when she'd been in a very similar situation. Then, she'd been a young mother with two children under the age of four, living in a tiny flat in the Birmingham suburb of Ladywood. She'd got the terrible news from the War Office that her first husband, Sergeant William Allman, was missing in action. During the early days of the Battle of the Somme, there'd been such an enormous number of casualties it would sometimes take several weeks, or more, before their next of kin could be notified. After waiting many long days, my mother had received the dreaded news to say he was no longer listed as missing – he'd been killed in action.

Sergeant Allman and my father had been mates in the same battery of the Royal Field Artillery in 1916. Dad was with him when he died.

Chapter Two: Preparations for War

June continued to slide away, and, although there were reports of stragglers turning up several days after the Dunkirk evacuation had been completed, there was no respite for my mother. Dad was still missing.

The fall of France brought with it a marked change in the attitude of civilians towards the possibility of air raids. Until then, like us, most of our neighbours hadn't bothered to check out their Anderson shelters since they'd been erected many months before. The public had been reasonably well informed of the horrors that had befallen many cities on the Continent, but didn't want to believe that they could be subjected to the same kind of terror. They liked to think they were different – they were British.

Some were known to be using their shelters to store garden tools and the like. Others had allowed their shelters to become cubby-holes for children to play in, while more than just a few shelters were now the venues for teenage romances, providing the ideal seclusion for a quiet kiss and a cuddle. There were a couple of our nearby neighbours who had initially thought the shelters were a waste of public money and showed their disapproval by not even bothering to have them erected, assumptions that turned out to be woefully wrong and had to be revised in haste a few weeks later.

At my mother's request, I'd reserved Sunday morning to heap more earth and turf on top of our shelter, then spent an hour bailing out water before realising I was fighting a losing battle. The bad news was, because of excessive seepage, there was always going to be at least eighteen inches of water in our shelter.

The day before, the amateur football team I played with had its final game of the season. Westfield, as we were known, had performed well throughout most of the winter, only falling away a little during March-April after losing three of our best players who'd enrolled in the forces. Their departure had strengthened my position in the team, where all the players were at least four or five years older than me, but there now seemed a possibility that, come September, Westfield might not even be able to field a side at all. One of our main rivals, Woodlands, was another South Birmingham team and, I must admit, they played better football than us right through the 1939-40 fixtures. Those two mates of mine who played for Woodlands would never have imagined me making such a statement.

At work the following Monday we made our second visit to the air raid shelter. The makeshift shelter comprised a series of long narrow tunnel-like cellars beneath the old four-storey factory building which been cleaned up a bit and given a coat of white-wash, before being fitted out with benches. The cellars had also been reinforced with heavy pine timber, some of this severely hampering movement. I dreaded the thought of having to evacuate the building in a hurry. Some of Webley's several hundred workers said they'd prefer to stay above ground, the main objections coming from machine operators on piecework because their pay was reduced somewhat when they were away from their machines.

By the middle of June, the war was beginning to loom large in our lives. Although the community's morale appeared to be still pretty high, even as a lad, I'd noticed that people were becoming more and more aware of the seriousness of our situation. This was most apparent in conversations among our neighbours and my mates at work. In recent weeks, the news had been all bad. Supply ships that the country was dependent upon were being torpedoed at an irreplaceable rate and the Luftwaffe was already flying reconnaissance missions over the whole of southern England. Most people were at last realising that the mock air raid alerts would soon become the real thing.

On Saturday, June 15, while out walking near Elmdon, I watched Bristol Blenheim aircraft of the RAF as they hedge-hopped across open fields before heading off in the direction of Coventry. I'd first seen this type of warplane at an air display two years earlier when I was a twelve-year-old, and could still remember how much I'd been impressed by them, so much so that I thought to myself, I pity those poor Germans if Hitler ever goes to war against us. Now, having heard what the Luftwaffe had done to Warsaw, Rotterdam, and other European cities, something told me the Germans were managing quite all right despite my earlier sentiments.

On Sunday morning, I kicked a ball around in the park near my home, something that for me in recent years had become a way of life. This was an opportunity to see my mates and catch up with some of the local gossip, and also served as a means of extending slightly the bounds of the very small world in which I'd so happily lived.

In recent weeks, there'd been plenty to talk about without even mentioning Aston Villa, the team that provided the inspiration for most of the local kids. That day the main topic was the urgent request the government had made for young men to enlist in the armed forces. Several of the lads thought it was inevitable that we would all be in the forces before long, and with the threat of a German invasion increasing by the hour, some decided they were going to answer the call. This way, they argued, there'd be a better chance of getting into a unit of their choice.

By Monday morning, my mother told me we'd got to face up to it: we were now unlikely to see Dad again until after the war. We could only assume he'd been taken prisoner by the Germans and that things were going to get worse, possibly much worse, before they would start to get any better.

At work that day, I'd found it hard to keep my mind on the job. With another two of my best team-mates enlisting, and my mother's fears about Dad, I was beginning to wonder what had happened to all those happy times we'd had before this blinking war started. The bus trip home that evening seemed different somehow; I had the feeling I'd suddenly become a stranger in my own town. There appeared to be so many more men in uniform now or maybe I just hadn't taken that much notice before. And the men who weren't in uniform had that tired drawn out look of being overworked and always needing to get home in a hurry, and hardly ever a smile. What's happening to everyone? I wondered.

I walked towards home after getting off the bus, and noticed a group of neighbours talking, which seemed a bit unusual at that time of day.

As I passed, they turned towards me with smiles.

'Did you have a good day, Joe?' said a jovial Mrs Heath.

What's going on? I thought but soon found out when I opened the front door and went inside.

There was a khaki greatcoat lying across the settee in the lounge. I immediately looked towards the kitchen, where my eyes met those of my mother.

'Yes, he's home. He arrived not long after you left for work this morning.'

'How is he, then? And what happened to him?'

'He looks good,' she said, 'but I'd better let your Dad tell you where he's been. There's no need for you to ask where he is now.'

I was shocked at the way Dad's unexpected arrival had affected my mother. She was pale, and her eyes gave the impression she had shed a few tears. I never liked to see Mum like that.

'Is it alright for me to take a look at Dad's rifle, do you think?'

'You'd better not, Joe,' she said. 'I think you'd better wait till morning and get your dad to show it to you.'

After tea I kicked a ball around with my friends until dark. Then while we talked on the way home from the park, our conversation was interrupted by the wail of air raid sirens.

A little closer to home, I heard a voice that I hadn't heard for ten months – the old man, on his way back from the pub. He must have been pretty full; he was looking up into the searchlight beams and telling the Germans just exactly what he thought of them in the most unrefined terms, attracting the attention of our close neighbours and bringing smiles to some of their faces. As there hadn't been any gun fire, the plane we could hear was probably one of our own.

Next morning I did get to look at Dad's rifle. The short magazine Lee-Enfield was much heavier than I'd expected and had been in service with the British Army since before the First World War. Now, as an apprentice of nearly four months with Webley and Scott, I'd got the impression the Lee-Enfield must have been one of the few old weapons used by the British Army in 1940 that had stood the test of time.

During breakfast Dad gave me a brief run-down of his exploits during the last week or so of his trek across France. He made it sound like a lot of fun and no doubt much of it had been. But there'd been a few awkward situations too, such as the time a few members of the French community at Saint Malo wanted to deny them the fishing boat on which they'd eventually managed to get away from France.

Many residents of Saint Malo had considered the war was now over as far as they were concerned; all they wanted was to get back to work and forget about it. Not surprisingly, there were objections to Dad and his men commandeering the boat on which other people's livelihood depended. Only the intervention of a local government official averted what might have turned into a nasty situation. According to Dad, their departure from Saint Malo and the trip back across the channel was a bit of an anti-climax following the exciting series of events that had enabled them to get back to England.

When asked if he'd encountered the Wehrmacht during his dash to avoid capture, he told me he'd always managed to keep just one jump ahead.

I think the sergeant major at the Gospel Oak got it right, his estimated two hours duration for Dad's assignment hadn't been quite long enough.

Dad's survivor's leave soon dwindled away. He spent most of it catching up with his mates. It was probably on the night of Tuesday, June 25, the evening before he had to return to his regiment, that an air raid alert sounded. My younger brother, Larry, and I stood in the back yard near our shelter. We found the night sky fascinating and had no idea Birmingham had the coverage of so many searchlights. My father arrived home that evening with the sad news that one of his close friends, a distant relative in fact, had lost his life on the *Lancastrian* when endeavouring to escape from France. The *Lancastrian* was a passenger liner that had been re-commissioned as a troopship. The ship, loaded to capacity, was dive-bombed and sunk by Stukas after the Luftwaffe had cunningly allowed the liner to clear Saint-Nazaire a number of miles before attacking. Dad's friend was one of several thousand soldiers who'd drowned. My father told us he could easily have been aboard the *Lancastrian*, as it had been touch and go whether his small detachment would leave from Saint Malo or Saint-Nazaire, about seventy miles further south. He said he should be counting his blessings. The next morning Dad was up early. I can still remember him telling me that our two trees looked like having a good crop of apples that year. He also seemed very serious when he complimented me, saying he reckoned I'd done a good job with the additional earth cover on our air raid shelter. His remarks left me with the feeling that those earlier plans he'd had to grow mushrooms in the shelter, for the time being at any rate, had suddenly been shelved. That morning, I said goodbye to him, not knowing that I wouldn't see my father again for almost four years. A month or two passed before we learned he was stationed in the Faeroe Islands, roughly halfway between the north of Scotland and Iceland, after having spent a short time in the Shetlands.

Hardly a month since Churchill's stirring speech of defiance, one could sense a resurgence of effort in all walks of life. My fellow employees at Webley and Scott were told they had to work longer hours. There seemed to be a greater willingness among the general public to take up voluntary duties such as fire watching and first aid, become air raid wardens or join the newly-formed Local Defence Volunteers, in addition to a big response from young men to the call to enlist in the armed forces. Another of my close friends, seventeen-year-old George Bowman, had left the week before to join the South Staffordshire Regiment. At this rate it looked as though very soon I'd be the only one in civvies in my little neck of the woods.

We got our first real look at the enemy the following Sunday morning while playing football in the park. I was amazed to see a twin-engine German aircraft almost directly overhead. It had been heading in the direction of the industrial suburbs of Tyseley and Small Heath. The aircraft was moving too fast and too high for me to make a positive identification. Our friendly game was quickly brought to a halt as we followed its path across the sky in a north-easterly direction, all the lads anticipating an expected response from our anti-aircraft batteries. The game then continued, but with a little less determination.

This incursion seemed strange to me because air raid sirens sounded several minutes after the intruder had passed but not one shot had been fired. Could it have been that gunners were told to hold their fire to conceal their positions from what had obviously been a reconnaissance mission by the Luftwaffe? Might it have been a breakdown of communications? A more likely reason. Or, was it feasible that the German visit may have passed unnoticed on account of the popularity of the Sunday morning sessions at the Gospel Oak?

August was only days away; the war would soon be entering its second year. Elements of the returned British Expeditionary Force had been deployed hastily over much of southern and south-eastern England, and despite the gravity of the situation, the morale of the armed forces appeared surprisingly high. The Churchill pugnacity was no doubt starting to rub off on our military leaders. We were beginning to think that perhaps, given six or twelve months grace to train, re-equip and begin modernising the army, we might yet be able to keep our home record intact.

We always knew it was eventually going to happen, and that night it did. Just when we'd thought it too late for enemy bombers to show up, the night sky was suddenly illuminated by dozens of searchlights. The tormenting wail of air raid sirens had created such a contrast to the beautiful songs of blackbirds we'd been admiring, while sitting out in the garden a little earlier that evening. It wasn't long before the haunting, uneven drone of enemy aircraft could be heard over a wide area, creating a situation that convinced my mother and brothers that the Anderson shelter was the place to be. I was starting to get impatient, I remember, because I couldn't understand why our gunners were holding their fire. Cripes, don't tell me they're waiting for the searchlights to find them a target.

Seconds later all hell broke loose. Many ack-ack shells were exploding directly above us, causing shrapnel to make weird sounds on its way down to earth as well as rattling and breaking tiles on the roof of our house. As the raid developed, it seemed to be directed more towards the city centre and the northern suburbs and we left our shelter briefly to talk to our neighbours across the garden fence.

Gunners from the battery up the road had been firing almost continuously since the raid started, while muzzle flashes from their guns created short spasms of daylight making it possible to move freely around the garden without the use of a torch, besides allowing us to wave to friends around their shelters several doors up the street.

A few miles to the north-east, parts of the city were ablaze, reflections from fires lighting up the night sky. German aircraft that approached Birmingham from the south were still getting fired on from our local battery, along with several others covering the southern half of the city.

But it was only when aircraft were being targeted above us that we needed to take cover. During quieter periods we stretched out on top of our shelter looking up into searchlight beams, hoping to see them pick up a bomber and a chance we might even see one shot down. The pattern of the raid varied little from the time of the alert until around one in the morning, when the last of the raiders appeared to have departed the Birmingham area, the all-clear sounding half an hour later. Then, all that remained was a strong smell of burning buildings, a golden-red glow in the sky to the north and, I imagined, tens of thousands of weary-eyed Brummies like us.

Daybreak saw the beginning of a new craze among children of all ages as they began roaming streets and parks in search of shrapnel from anti-aircraft shells. There were boys and girls as young as four or five, all hoping to be able to claim the biggest piece of shrapnel or any other relic, as mementoes of our first real raid. As for me, there was still the water problem in our shelter to be attended to. We'd found out during the raid that one would need to be a contortionist to occupy a bunk in our shelter without getting wet.

During the bus trip to work on Monday there was more than the normal amount of interest shown by passengers. We'd heard there were large areas of devastation near the city centre and that it might be a slow trip into town.

By the time I got to work, I'd seen little evidence of this. There were fire crews about, some of them hosing down roads, but I did manage to get to work on time as any bomb damage had been well away from the bus route. When I arrived at Webley's I learned more about the raid, for some of the toolroom staff had been much closer to the action.

One of them, a gauge grinder named Francis, brought in a large piece of bomb shrapnel that he'd found embedded in brickwork on the side of his house, and before we were told to get on with it by our foreman, Harry Sharp, it was generally felt that the raid was most likely an exploratory one.

We all agreed we could expect the raids to get progressively worse as the threatened invasion drew closer, and the many prophets of the toolroom were soon to be proven correct.

Two or three nights later enemy bombers were back. This time the raid seemed to be directed at targets closer to my home. The first raiders came in from the south-west, releasing a string of chandelier flares as they crossed the southern suburbs. The ack-ack seemed to be a lot more concentrated than our first raid and the noise intensity deafening. Shortly after, more bombers were fired on, we heard the thud and felt the strong vibrations from bombs detonating. My mother and Larry were arguing as to whether or not they were bombs we'd heard. I think Mum knew they were bombs but must have thought it best for my brother to believe otherwise. Twelve-year-old Larry attended Yardley Grammar School, where our older brother, John, had also been a student. The build-up of raids during the following weeks must have made it easier for my mother to consent to Larry being evacuated along with the rest of his class to the safety of the Elan Valley in Wales.

We were entering the second half of August. Air raids were now becoming the main reason for getting home from work in a hurry each evening, in the hope you might finish tea before the bombs began to fall. The threat of invasion must have presented the government with its biggest headache. More calls for volunteers came each day and there were many young men finding it hard to sit back while such a crisis existed. As the days passed, we found ourselves spending more time in the shelter than in the house.

The water problem made things pretty miserable in our shelter. It was so cramped that it was hard to keep our feet above the water level. There was an old potato sack hung across the entrance and this served to hold in the light of one candle-power, the candle providing enough light for us to see each other's eyes, and very little else.

Following a raid alert, gun fire could be heard in the distance, a few searchlights pointing to the south-east indicating action was most likely heading our way. We took to the shelter. During heavy gun fire about fifteen minutes later, the demoralising scream of a bomb close by caused us to freeze momentarily while fearfully awaiting the detonation. The shock waves that accompanied the explosion made our shelter vibrate somewhat and sent a faint ripple across the water as falling dust all but snuffed out the candle.

There was then a short silence: even Mum wasn't game to try to pass that one off as gun fire. Instead, she said it must have been a long way away, to which I remember Larry replying, 'You've got to be kidding, Mum.'

'If your Dad was here I'm sure he'd be able to explain,' she told him.

The raid went on. Other bombs were exploding but seemed a little further away. By half-past-two in the morning we were able to creep back into the house and, surprisingly, got some sleep.

Not long after daybreak Larry and I decided to take a look at the bomb site. We knew it must have been quite close and in just a couple of minutes we'd found it. The bomb had detonated just around the corner on Wildfell Road and here we got our first real glimpse at the horror of war. We stood close up to what was hardly more than a huge heap of rubble, but in actual fact we were looking over all that remained of a block of two-storey semi-detached homes.

We were amazed that a solitary bomb had caused so much devastation. A classmate of Larry's had been living in one of the homes destroyed and immediately opposite lived Nobby Humphries, who was a footballing mate and whose younger sister, Hazel, had been a friendly classmate of mine just a couple of years earlier. We stood and watched civil defence crews as they searched among the huge mound of debris, before learning from other bystanders that there must have been a heavy loss of life.

Soon we were to learn that Larry's schoolmate and the rest of his family had been in their shelter, and that the bomb had exploded between their home and the shelter. It looked as though no one could have survived. We didn't hang around too long as there was nothing we could do to help.

My mother didn't say much when we told her what we'd seen. She'd known the parents of several of the families who'd lived in the block. What really disturbed Mum, I think, was that Larry's schoolmate and his family had been in their shelter when the bomb struck, casting doubts on the misguided belief she'd held regarding the degree of safety provided by that water-logged hole in the ground in our backyard. Mum's safety beliefs would be further strained a few months later after she learned about another Anderson shelter, one the same as ours.

A bomb had lifted it out of a garden in Avenue Road in the suburb of Aston, sending it flying over the roofs of neighbouring homes before finishing up in a heap of twisted metal on an adjacent street.

During breakfast that morning, my mother appeared deep in thought. She was well aware the nights would soon be getting longer and colder and this would make the small hardships we'd experienced in recent weeks seem like the good times.

When I arrived home from work on Monday, the good news was that government sub-contractors would soon be putting concrete bases in water-logged shelters like ours, eliminating the seepage problem. They might take a while, Mum was told, but they had plans to try to fix our shelter before the winter set in. The proposed waterproofing was the topic of our discussions in the shelter that night, as we debated the way in which the contractors would have to tackle the problem. The gun fire was heavy. The raid was possibly our biggest to date.

We were starting to feel as though we might at last be learning to live with the pantomime that took place during the hours of darkness each night. We no longer flinched at the thunder or flashes from guns. As for the bombs, we'd learned that if we could hear them coming down we most likely would be all right, the limited experience we'd had led us to believe that in all probability they were destined to explode somewhere else. Even the bunks in the shelter were starting to feel a little softer. The fact of the matter was, that, after weeks of sleepless nights we were all too tired for those little discomforts to register any more.

There was no need to worry if you thought you didn't look your usual bright self when catching the bus for work each morning – everyone else was in the same boat, and to comment on the night's raid was always a quick way to open a conversation. Some of my favourite girlfriends were among the ones I'd first met while travelling on a four-penny workman's return following a night in the shelter. Trips into the city each morning became mystery tours, the bus having to leave its regular route on umpteen occasions, some roads being sealed off to keep traffic away from UXBs or DAs (unexploded or delayed-action bombs).

Other roads had still to be cleared of rubble, particularly within a mile or so around the Stratford and Warwick Road intersection. The extent of bomb damage was now becoming more evident and we often passed rescue teams who'd been working throughout the night. This was a scene that had become the norm: men clambering over the ruins of buildings while ambulances stood close by with rear doors open in anticipation.

The bomb damage was now becoming such that each morning I expected to arrive at work to find a heap of rubble where the factory once stood. The way the raids were intensifying, the prospects of this happening now seemed a real possibility.

In recent weeks it was as though we were living in two different worlds, one that during the hours of daylight, except for the worst areas of devastation, people went about their business as though we weren't at war. Then, half an hour after sunset each evening we'd anxiously await the transition that followed an air raid alert, usually bringing with it weird sounds accompanied by lighting effects that could realistically add fitting characterisations to a Charles Gounod opera. The stressful hours of darkness were indeed another world.

It was good to get to work, if only to hear how my workmates from other parts of the city were coping. Their spirits always seemed high, and they often had interesting stories to tell. In fact, some of their stories were quite comical, resulting in loud laughter around the toolroom. This, I can still clearly remember, was much to the displeasure of our foreman, Harry Sharp. The biggest concern of my workmates – especially some of the older ones – was the threat of invasion. They'd heard that Hitler had recently ordered his military chiefs to complete preparations for the invasion of England.

There was an air of apprehension hanging over the country, particularly in the south-east. My elder brother John, who was sixteen, had applied to join the RAF. But unlike the Army, the RAF and the Navy insisted potential recruits produce birth certificates on enlistment. Because he'd been too young at the time and wanted aircrew training, they'd taken his particulars and told him they would send for him. John would have to spend at least another year at home with Mum, leaving the way open for me to enlist in the army.

And so, on September 19, 1940, at the age of fourteen, I resolved to answer the call to enlist in the army. This decision was arrived at during a routine football session with my mates in the park. Although they were all a few years older, they convinced me I'd have a good chance of getting past the recruiter.

Apart from the army being desperate for recruits, we'd also heard that should we enlist during the following two weeks we would almost certainly be enrolled in a battalion of the Dorsetshire Regiment. This was the unit where a couple of our teammates were already serving.

Churchill had told the nation that we'd fight them on the beaches, among many other places, and that sounded like a good idea at that time. The general feeling was that, unless we could defeat an invasion attempt before the Germans were able to establish a bridgehead in the south of England, the war for us would almost certainly be lost. Quite apart from that, the thought of living under Nazi occupation made the decision to enlist much easier.

Britain's very loyal, but now so obviously outdated armed forces, particularly the army, were spread around the globe in the summer of 1940, but it was here in Britain where they'd suddenly become most needed. But since my juvenile appearance could add to the possibility of the recruiter not accepting me, I decided not to resign my apprenticeship at Webley and Scott immediately.

Chapter Three: Enlistment Day

My imagination was in overdrive as I sat a little restless and somewhat deep in thought on a bus heading into the city. Surprisingly, it wasn't the recruiting office that was foremost in my thoughts; instead my mind was preoccupied trying to visualise the 9 a.m. scene around the toolroom at Webley's without my presence. Wednesday, September 18, will be the first time foreman Sharp would be placing a cross beside the name of his lone apprentice.

A little later, expert toolmaker and top universal miller exponent, Ernie Harris, will take a casual glance towards the clock with a sigh. He will by then be aware that, come twelve o'clock he'll be making his own way to the pub on Snow Hill, that's if he decides to have the usual ham sandwich for his lunch. At least the correct amount of hot mustard will be to Ernie's liking today.

Arriving at the recruiting office I made a couple of brief enquiries before joining a long queue of mainly happy-looking but anxious young men, and got the feeling most of them must have come from Birmingham's poorer suburbs, areas that had only recently begun recovering from the sad years of the world depression.

Ironically it seemed fate had chosen them along with many thousands of others around Britain in order to boost the numbers of much needed servicemen, and I must admit, I just couldn't quite imagine that one day in the future some of these hopefuls were going to be the ones given the mammoth task of hanging out the washing on the Siegfried Line.

The queue of soon-to-be servicemen was moving fairly quickly, giving an impression of extreme urgency. Less than half an hour later I stood at a table where a very business-like middle-aged woman sat, her hands delving briskly into heaps of documents. She didn't bother to look up at me when asking several questions including my name, age and address. I'd decided to say I was nineteen. Then, still without looking up, she handed me a slip of paper with one hand and directed me to one of several nearby doors with the other. This was going to be easy I told myself. Had I two heads I don't think she would have noticed. Cripes, maybe the situation's even more desperate than we've been led to believe.

My next encounter was with one of several doctors, and after watching their procedure for a minute or two concluded they must have all been on piecework – I'd never seen medicos moving so quickly. After stripping, I waited just a couple of minutes before the next doctor, an elderly gentleman, became available. He looked me over a little inquisitively before going through a perfunctory routine, starting with my eyes, ears and breathing, then getting me to stand on one leg before checking my reflexes. Finally he asked me to give a firm cough, after which he asked my age. When I told him nineteen, he said, 'You're alright, you must be one of those late developers – it's OK to get dressed now.'

Once more I found myself at the tail of a queue, this one moving slowly towards a big fellow in uniform sitting at a desk. His mildly upright posture seemed overflowing with authority, while his colourful appearance would have looked quite in order had he been standing at the main entrance to Harrods. When there were just four fellows ahead of me, I could see his red and gold sergeant's stripes neatly tacked on his impeccable navy-blue uniform. He must have been about six foot three, with his waxed moustache complementing ribbons from the Great War displayed on his barrel chest.

After I'd looked the sergeant over from a closer distance, I felt for the first time since discussing my military future with my footballing mates in the park, that Joe Lake's prospects of becoming a soldier were no sure thing. Very soon there were just two fellows ahead of me. I was close enough to hear the questions being put to them before they were asked to stand and take the Oath of Allegiance. Then, after signing, each was given an attestation payment of four shillings and sixpence. At last, I thought, I'm about to become a few bob richer and can consider myself a member of His Majesty's Armed Forces. Not necessarily in that order, of course.

'Well, me lad. What branch of the service have you decided on?' the sergeant asked. Then, as he closely scrutinised me and my papers, he nodded. 'Oh, yes, so you've settled for the army, then, have you, lad?'

He looked me over curiously with his head tilted slightly to one side. I got the feeling that he may have been trying to visualise me standing there rigged out in full marching order. He paused for a few moments.

'Very well then, there's just one other thing before I get you to sign. What's your present occupation?'

'Tool-making,' I told him. 'I'm an apprentice toolmaker with Webley and Scott.' He seemed to welcome my reply. He didn't actually smile, but I thought I may have detected relief on his face.

'Oh dear!' he said. 'That's a reserved occupation. Surely you're aware of that? Look, I'm very sorry lad, but we aren't allowed to enrol a person who's in a reserved occupation.'

I quickly recovered from this unexpected shock he'd cast on me and explained that I had plans to join friends in the Dorsetshire Regiment, and that, perhaps he could make just one exception.

'You know, at Webley and Scott,' I told him, 'it's generally acknowledged that it takes about fifteen years before anyone could seriously consider themselves to be an accomplished toolmaker. And, without trying to appear too melodramatic, as you well know, we've been led to believe the destiny of this country may be decided in the next fifteen weeks.'

He looked me squarely in the face.

'Look lad, had you arrived here telling me you were a window cleaner or something in that order, then I most likely could have taken you.' I immediately sensed he was offering me some sort of direction. I paused briefly to allow my heartbeat to get back to somewhere near normal again, before smiling. 'OK, I'm a window cleaner.' I said, expecting him to invite me to sign on the dotted line.

'Oh no, I can't accept that now. You've already stated otherwise. Look, I'm sorry but I'm afraid I'm going to have to ask you to move on,' he told me. 'You're holding up the queue. If you happen to be around this way some other time, we probably will be taking window cleaners.' His roundabout way of proceeding seemed a bit stupid to me at the time, but the following day when I arrived back at the recruiting depot, it took little more than thirty minutes for me to get the four and sixpence that had eluded me less than twenty-four hours earlier.

The sergeant looked me over as though he'd never seen me before. He put to me much the same questions that he'd done on my first visit. For all I know he may have already had "window cleaner" down on my papers when he saw me approaching his desk and he certainly didn't harp too long on the subject of my contrived occupation. At the end of the proceedings, and after telling me what a fine regiment the Dorsetshires was, he wished me good luck, before turning to greet the next recruit.

In spite of all the messing around, I hadn't considered the sergeant to be a bad sort of a fellow really. Looking back now, I'm pretty sure he probably wanted to satisfy himself that my enthusiasm was strong enough to bring me back next day.

And so around midday on Friday, September 20, 1940, I found myself about to board a train at Birmingham's New Street Station, pleased with the thought that after a little perseverance I'd managed to narrowly scrape through the first stage of becoming a soldier. On the platform I manoeuvred myself among the large crowd that had gathered to farewell relatives and friends. Many seemed to be in a particularly jovial mood and appeared to have made last-minute departures from city pubs. I'd felt a little insignificant as I weaved my way through them, carefully protecting the brown-paper bag that I had securely tucked under my arm. It hadn't bothered me that no one had been able to come along to see me off at the station; in a way I'd felt a bit like the old man, as far as I knew, his departure had also been a quiet one, after a couple of drinks with his mates at the Dolphin in Acock's Green.

As the train drew slowly from the platform, it was leaving behind a crowd that seemed a little bewildered, no doubt, because of the uncertainty of the times with many wondering how long it would be before they'd meet again. For me, I now faced the question of what the army might have in store.

I was leaving Brum with the satisfaction of knowing my brother John would be taking good care of my mother and that younger brother Larry would soon be evacuated to the Elan Valley in Wales. Before leaving home I'd been able to convince Mum, I thought, that my decision was one that although far from having Captain Oates' sacrifice in mind, would certainly be making things easier for the rest of the family. They would no longer have to sit on bunks in the shelter with their feet dangling in water, and soon elder brother John could also sleep in the shelter. These expectations appeared to have made my mother a little happier.

When being told that I'd be on the train for at least four hours, I was hoping there'd be a few young chaps to natter with during the trip, but this wasn't the case; all the passengers in my compartment were older. Many of the fellows were travelling light, most likely on missions the same as my own. I can still clearly remember how magnificent the countryside looked just a few miles out of Birmingham as I'd never had the pleasure of seeing it from a railway carriage before.

This rekindled happy memories of a two-week camping holiday during the summer of 1939 when I'd biked it to Ross-on-Wye with half a dozen classmates from school. Unfortunately, propelling my Dad's very old "sit up and beg" type roadster, heavily laden with camping gear and supplies, had proven to be too exhausting for me to really appreciate the beauty of the landscape.

Those two glorious weeks of the August holiday were spent at a lovely spot – where lack of funds had forced us to camp a little off the beaten track amidst dairy cattle and only a few feet from the edge of the swirling River Wye. This was my first and only time away from Birmingham and the Wye Valley seemed such a wonderful place. I think I could have stayed there forever and this despite having had to live on a shoe-string the first week. And how could I have ever forgotten the second week, our diet consisting almost entirely of cheaply acquired apples and plums. To this day, there are times when my thoughts pleasantly wander back to the beautiful Wye Valley, this made possible on occasions I think, with a little reminder from Edward Elgar.

The LMS Express finally pulled into the busy Salisbury station, arriving a little late. After reporting to the Railway Transport Officer and then hanging around for a couple of hours, I was eventually ushered, along with six or seven other fellows, to an awaiting truck and in a matter of twenty minutes off-loaded at Skew Bridge, just out of Salisbury on the Wilton Road.

The camp that was to become my home for the next two months was situated on what had been the Wiltshire County Cricket Ground prior to its requisition by the War Department. It consisted of half a dozen marquees, fifty or sixty bell tents, and some semi permanent buildings comprising cookhouses and ablutions blocks.

Because we'd arrived late we were taken straight to the mess tent and given a meal, then to one of the marquees where we were handed a couple of blankets and a straw-filled palliasse and told we would be kitted out in the morning. The light was fading; it was close to darkness when I pulled over the blankets.

As I lay on my back with my hands supporting my head, I found myself listening to the strange accents of some of the other thirty or forty recruits who were spending their first night in the army under canvas. There was also an impromptu one-man concert taking place, the soloist a talented young chap from the Black Country who had the inappropriate name of Jimmy Howells. Jimmy was also spending his first night away from home. He had a remarkable voice and after each song was happy to sing personal requests, his versatility enabling him to do justice to the wide variety of songs he was called upon to perform.

Before finally falling asleep that first night in camp, I'd listened to "Begin the Beguine", "Yours", "Sierra Sue", "Maria Elena", "Broken-hearted Clown", "Amapola" and many more. I vaguely remember dozing off to what seemed like a slightly sentimental rendering of "Mexically Rose" and thinking: how lucky can I be, I've actually joined a unit with its own Chick Henderson.

During the following weeks I got to know Jimmy very well and found him a most likeable fellow, one of the many nice blokes I met during my time in the army.

On Saturday morning I awoke shortly before the bugler gave his version of Reveille, which to me seemed very good, as was his call to the cookhouse about an hour later preceding a fine breakfast. I knew it was early days but I remember thinking to myself: if this is the way the army lives, what with best New Zealand butter on the table along with two rashers of bacon for breakfast, it seems pretty good to me.

There didn't appear to be any great urgency regarding our next task which was to visit the quartermaster's store, in this case the drill hall situated a few hundred yards down the road towards Salisbury. This was where it took less than ten minutes for young men from the Brummagem area to be converted into private soldiers of the Dorsetshire Regiment.

We were to learn later that there was a delay in the supply of rifles and light machine guns, and that priority had been given to re-equipping units that had recently returned from Dunkirk. Our weapons would become available soon.

Later that day, we were advised by the paymaster that if we wished, we could make allowances to our families. This I was happy to do. From the two shillings a day that I would be receiving for the following six months, Mum would receive nine pence. Mum would get five shillings and three-pence a week and I would get the remaining eight shillings and nine-pence. That afternoon I was re-located from a marquee to one of the bell tents, which I shared with seven others. The tent was a bit crowded, but not too bad. My main problem was that most of the other chaps were from the Black Country and because of their accents I could hardly understand a word they said.

Our training over the next two weeks was limited due to the lack of equipment and this led to extra physical training sessions including route marches, cross-country runs, boxing and unarmed combat. On one of the following days our training included rifle drill, but because there were only about thirty obsolete rifles available for more than two hundred troops, the instruction period was brief. These particular rifles, known as EY rifles, were leftovers from the trench fighting days of the First World War. The stocks on the very old 303s had been reinforced with bound and soldered copper wire to enable them to discharge grenades, making them as heavy as they were unpopular.

News that Birmingham had been heavily targeted by the Luftwaffe over the last few nights was spreading around the camp. Also, there were rumours that weekend passes were to become available in the coming weeks, as well as buses to the Midlands for those who could afford the fare.

A few days later, the cross-country run was to be the longest we'd yet had to tackle and everyone in camp who wasn't gainfully employed had been ordered to front the starter.

About two o'clock on a bright sunny afternoon over two hundred of us headed off in the direction of the village of Dinton. After we'd covered a mile or so the runners were well strung out. We'd gone a little more than three miles when the leaders crossed the River Nadder and headed back towards camp. Shortly after, a corporal physical training instructor on a pushbike drew alongside and told me he thought I had a good chance of winning the race, even though there were at least fifty runners a fair way ahead.

'Is there anything for the winner?' I asked jokingly, not wanting to appear too mercenary.

'There's bound to be,' he replied.

So, with the thought of a few bob in my sights, which I could put towards a weekend bus trip home, I raised the tempo a little and soon found myself passing other runners, some of them in groups and actually holding conversations as they ran. When there were only a few runners ahead and roughly a mile to the finish, the corporal physical training instructor once more appeared at my side.

'You've won it,' he said. 'We're almost there.'

'But what about him?' I asked. 'That fellow who's thirty or forty yards way out in front and still cruising along as if the run had just started.'

'Oh him, don't worry about him, he's the Sergeant PTI. He just came along as the pacemaker. You're the winner. I'd better get your name.'

That day was very rewarding for me. And not just for the packet of twenty Players cigarettes the orderly officer of the day presented me with for winning the race. This victory, minor as it had been, gave me a much greater feeling of satisfaction.

Not long after leaving home, while on the train in fact, I'd secretly asked myself whether I would be able to perform well enough among "grown-ups" to justify the decision I'd made to enlist.

In the back of my mind was the fear that the army would suddenly pounce on me and ask, Who'd you think you're kidding? before telling me to get back into my civvies and head off back to Brummagem. Winning the race gave me the feeling there was a good possibility that I would now be OK.

The actual race had not been a problem for me because I'd done a lot of running and knew that I was pretty fit. Against the wishes of my parents, and to spend more time with my school mates, I'd delivered newspapers morning and evening six days a week from the age of ten until leaving school a couple of weeks before my fourteenth birthday.

The morning delivery was often done at the double to avoid being late for school. Aside from that, living in the particular part of Birmingham where I grew up, kids who were quick off the mark found it much easier to keep out of trouble.

There was a little more enemy air activity reported during the next few days causing a few casualties. Marauding German aircraft had strafed several camps across Salisbury Plain and this prompted Company Sergeant Major Trusler to get the men digging trenches along the tent line near the camp boundary. We had seen German aircraft generally moving fast and very high, most likely on photographic reconnaissance missions in conjunction with Hitler's planned invasion.

But, as there was a strong RAF presence in this part of southern England, the Luftwaffe wasn't a big problem, especially during daylight hours. The trench digging proved to be hard going. The ground was a reddish loam that contained a very high amount of a white shale or chalky substance, possibly limestone. My hands weren't the only ones that got badly blistered before the CSM finally called it a day.

After a couple of weeks in camp I began to question the sense of urgency that had led to my enlistment. I'd been expecting to arrive at some strategic spot in the south-east of England near the coast, where I'd have been immediately thrown into the preparation of defences and generally striving to make up for lost time.

We'd been led to believe this was necessary if we were to have any hope of thwarting the threatened German invasion. Since arriving at Salisbury it was pretty clear to me that I must have misinterpreted the seriousness of the calls that the government had made for recruits. At that point in time the main emphasis of our training was on fitness.

Among the few things I'd learned was how to salute a commissioned officer by numbers, basic first aid, the importance of personal hygiene, as well as recognising the differences in the many bugle calls we heard between reveille and lights out. And, oh yes, a brief history of the Dorsetshire Regiment.

From some of the "old" soldiers in camp I'd also learned how important it was to make sure that you were always on friendly terms with the company storeman, and that it was only under very special circumstances that you'd ever be silly enough to volunteer for anything. I was also reminded that a little properly applied "bull" would more than likely help to baffle the brains of my superiors. To me this hardly seemed the kind of thinking that was going to help turn back the hordes of Huns!

At my age I was still very conscientious and in no position to kid myself that I understood the big picture of what was going on in the troubled world outside the camp. Come to think of it, I hadn't known too much about what was going on inside the camp, for that matter.

Another thought also occurred to me about that time. I'd began to wonder if perhaps I'd have been doing the country a greater service had I continued to play my part in the production of Rolls-Royce Merlins at Webley and Scott.

On Saturday, a mate and I decided to visit Salisbury and, to save the cost of a bus ticket, we walked into town. I found it strange to hear the sound of hobnail boots on a hard surface as this was my first liberty venture out of camp.

The town centre was very much alive with military personnel, many from overseas such as Australians, New Zealanders, Canadians, Indians and others. A small crowd of sightseers had congregated near a corner of the town's market square to gloat over an enemy bomber. The Dornier had fallen into our hands intact and was put on display there.

As we joined the many onlookers, we listened to a tune we thought must have been the popular Joe Loss version of "In the Mood" coming from a milkbar close by. We entered the milkbar, and a pleasant and very attractive teenage girl served me my first-ever milkshake (rum flavoured) and told us that we'd actually been listening to the American, Glenn Miller. Although we'd got it wrong, that Miller recording was a pleasant talking point, and a copy of it remains in my collection today.

Next day, we paraded to get our newly arrived rifles. This turned out to be a bitter disappointment after finding we weren't getting Lee-Enfields. Instead, we got old American P-14s, of First World War vintage. They were ugly and heavy. Cripes, I thought, you'd really need to be a six-footer to handle these weapons with bayonets fixed.

'No, no, no! They couldn't have been,' two Brummies argued towards the back of our squad. 'Don't show your blinking ignorance – the Alamo was ages ago I tell you, you don't know what you're talking about.'

Our company commander said he understood and shared our feelings, but reminded us that beggars couldn't be choosers. On the plus side, we were surprised to find out on the rifle range a few days later that in the right hands, these weapons were very accurate.

At bayonet practice the following week our sergeant major happened to be standing close by when I ferociously thrust my bayonet into a straw-filled sack that represented an unfortunate enemy soldier.

The CSM looked a bit surprised at the harsh language I'd used as I savagely drove in the bayonet – language that our instructor encouraged us to use to whip up aggression. They were words that weren't completely new to me, but they'd certainly not been part of my vocabulary until I'd started bayonet practice.

'That's the idea, Lake,' remarked the CSM. 'I take it you must really hate those Germans.'

I made no response. I could have pointed out that in recent years, apart from Germany occupying a couple of pages in my stamp album, Germany and the Germans had hardly ever entered my thoughts at all, but deemed it wiser not to say anything.

On a cold morning late in October, fog blanketed most of the camp until 10 a.m. showing early signs of the approaching winter, and the whole camp area was becoming soggy underfoot.

That afternoon, much to my dismay, we were confronted with a snap kit inspection that found me to be deficient of one greatcoat. Our quartermaster was quick to let me know that the cost of a replacement coat would be three pounds ten shillings, ruling out any hope I had for a trip home to see Mum for a long time. Luckily, I hadn't hinted to her to expect to see me home soon.

On Friday's pay parade, I saluted the officer at the pay table and was shocked when the quartermaster advised the pay clerk to give me one shilling.

'Is there some mistake here?' inquired the attending officer, as he whispered, 'Surely we can't expect a soldier to manage the week on one shilling?'

'Unfortunately, I'm afraid that's the way it is, sir,' said the quartermaster. 'He gets the shilling to buy soap and boot polish, leaving no excuse for him to get on parade untidy.'

'I see,' said the orderly officer, 'and what did Private Lake do to get into this situation?'

'He lost his greatcoat,' replied the QM. 'Like I said, it's unfortunate, but he's responsible for his kit so he has to pay.'

I wasn't over consoled when the quartermaster did point out to the orderly officer that overcrowding in some tents made it almost impossible to keep track of personal possessions.

Lack of funds was one reason I stayed in camp that day. It was also cold and wet. Mid afternoon I ventured down to the ablutions block in a bid to find a spot a bit warmer than the tent. There I found Eddie Atkinson sitting under a shower, a steady trickle of hot water enveloping him in vapour.

'How are you, Eddie? How long have you been here?' I asked, as I began stripping off.

'About an hour or so,' he told me. 'It's the only place in camp where I can keep warm.'

Eddie, who came from the Birmingham suburb of Small Heath, arrived in camp the day after me and we'd been good friends since. One of our few differences was that Eddie lived near St Andrews football ground and as you'd expect, was a Birmingham City supporter, whereas I had always been a follower of Aston Villa. Eddie and I had a few chats during the following weeks while sitting in the showers, but as the colder weather began to set in, our sub-tropical retreat attracted a bigger following, so much so that the camp hot-water system failed to cope with the demand.

The news was all bad from Birmingham. While London was making the headlines since becoming the prime target of the Luftwaffe in recent weeks, raids on Birmingham had continued nightly, some of the attacks closer to my house. Fellows returning from weekend bus trips had kept us up to date with the Blitz.

A friend who was back from the last trip said there'd been huge fires in Birmingham's city centre, and particularly around the main railway stations. This was the kind of news I didn't want to hear, especially since it was going to be at least three or four months before I'd be able to save enough money for the bus fare home.

Over the next few days I'd given quite a lot of thought to hitchhiking home. In camp it was common knowledge most motorists were very co-operative when men in uniform thumbed a lift. Unfortunately, hitching left too much to chance to be sure of getting back to camp on time. The thought of losing more pay for being absent without leave while still trying to pay off the missing greatcoat scotched that idea.

Light rain was falling when I made my way to the mess tent for breakfast. Mist hung across the lower part of the camp near the cookhouse, making another dismal start to the day. On a brighter note, one of the regular soldiers sitting at our table was of the opinion that we would have to evacuate the cricket ground soon. He told us there was a date set, limiting how long we were allowed to be under canvas in the UK, and that to comply with army regulations, we would have to move out of this camp very soon.

I thought he may have been overlooking the fact that we were now at war. The camp had become a quagmire and soon we would have to get boards in our tents to keep bedding off the damp ground.

Walking back from the mess tent, I was able to speak to Peter Vandermin, who was one of the occupants of an adjacent tent. Peter had heard of my misfortune regarding the greatcoat and told me that he too had been a victim of petty theft. However, in his case it had been mainly knives and forks. Peter was something of odd man out in this unit. He'd obviously come from a very wealthy family, which would almost certainly have made him a one-off in our company. From others I'd learned that Peter had arrived at the main gate in a chauffeur driven Rolls Royce, and this only a few hours before I'd arrived carrying the paper bag that contained my toothbrush and most of my worldly possessions.

Anyone listening to him speak would have realised immediately that Peter came from the other end of town and was well educated. Why would he want to waste his talents in an infantry unit like this one? Patriotism was the common denominator that Peter shared with most others in the camp. He was well liked among all ranks, and knowing his background, most of the blokes thought he must have been making a bigger sacrifice than the rest of us. No one had ever heard Peter complain.

Sergeant Major Trusler poked his head into our tent just after breakfast. He seemed concerned about the deteriorating weather and its affect on the tent dwellers.

'Have you had a trip home yet, Lake?' he muttered, as he moved quickly to the next tent, showing little interest in my disheartened reply. I think he was probably well aware of my grim financial situation.

Late that afternoon, Peter Vandermin wanted to know if I planned a trip into Salisbury that evening, then asked if I'd mind picking up a couple of items for him.

I hadn't intended going into Salisbury, but thought I could use the opportunity to stamp some of the mud off my boots, and return a favour to Peter who'd been good to me in one way and another.

There was no surprise when Peter asked if I'd bring him back a knife and fork. This was a consequence of the procedure used at the YMCA canteen in Salisbury. There, anyone requesting a meal that required a knife and fork was asked to leave a shilling deposit on each item, this they got back when the utensils were returned.

Not surprisingly, for soldiers who were paid two shillings a day, knives and forks soon became currency. A soldier who was skint, and after Saturday most of them were, would take his army-issued knife and fork to the

YMCA canteen, claim a two-shilling deposit and then go to the pictures or down a couple of pints. As a result, the YMCA canteen staff – who may have been turning a blind eye to the practice – always had a huge pile of cutlery, while back in camp one or two of my colleagues tried not to make it too obvious that they were eating all their meals with a spoon.

On my return from Salisbury, I quietly gave the merchandise to Peter, knowing how he liked to keep a low profile with this kind of transaction. He offered me my bus fare, but after telling him that I'd walked to Salisbury, asked if he would care to lend me ten bob instead.

His response was, 'Very well then, Lake, but only on condition you promise me you definitely won't tell anyone.'

The next morning after breakfast I was able to add my name to the list of passengers for the trip north on Friday night. Unfortunately, there'd been insufficient time to let my mother know the good news.

Eddie Atkinson and I volunteered to work in the cookhouse next day, just as we'd done on a couple of other occasions. It was warm in the cookhouse and there was always a bucket of "sergeant major's" tea at hand, the quality of which easily had the edge on that sold in the NAAFI canteen, quite apart from the price being right. There was also the added attraction of a couple of hours off in the afternoon.

When the sun broke through around two o'clock, Eddie and Kenny Baggot, another Brummie, decided to join me for a walk into Salisbury. There, while crossing the market square near the German bomber, I was confronted by a very smart good-looking fellow who might well have been taking a short spell away from the Foreign Office. He wore a bowler and what looked like a Saville Row suit while carrying an umbrella and briefcase. When he spoke to me, my mates quietly slipped away into the background. But they didn't take their eyes off me.

'Don't I know you?' said this chap, and it was only then that I realised who he was. He was a gentleman by the name of Upton who at that time lived in Mirfield

Road, Solihull, less than two hundred yards from the clubhouse of the Olton Golf Club. He was a club member where, until a couple of months before, I'd been a part-time caddie. I hadn't ever seen him out of his golfing gear before.

He told me how he'd recently spoken to young navy friends of mine, Norman Holloway and Bertie Withy, who lived a short distance up the road from me and had been full-time caddies at Olton. (Both these teenagers were to have their lives cut short with the sinking of the battleships *Repulse* and *Prince of Wales* off Malaya on December 10, 1941.)

Before departing, he very kindly gave me a few bob and wished me good luck.

After he'd gone, Eddie and Ken quickly reappeared. 'What did he want?' they asked.

'What did you tell him?'

'Who was he?'

'What was that he gave you?'

'You didn't tell him anything did you?'

I had to tell them to calm down. 'He's from home, a very nice fellow too. I've known him since my caddying days at the Olton Golf Club.'

'We thought he might have been a member of the Fifth Column,' Ken remarked, 'especially when we saw him dive his hand into his pocket and then give you something.'

'Actually, he did ask me one thing about my unit,' I told them. 'He wanted to know how I'd come to be in the Dorsetshire Regiment, telling me I should have been in the Warwicks.'

By Friday morning, the rain had stopped. A light mist covered most of the camp, but the bleakness of the day couldn't dampen my enthusiasm. I was going home. The night before, I'd slept with my best pair of slacks under the palliasse and they looked pretty good when I made up my bed. My battledress blouse was crumpled slightly but this was unavoidable, living as we were in crowded tents. Roll on 4.30 so that I can get out of this place. I was really looking forward to being somewhere where there'd be a bit more elbow room.

About four o'clock that afternoon, all spick and span, after managing to scrounge a dab of Brylcreem from one of my Black Country colleagues in the tent, and feeling more than a little optimistic, I ventured down to the cookhouse in the hope that I could get something to take home for my mother. The cooks were hard at it preparing the evening meal, but I managed to approach the corporal cook and asked if he would let me have something I could take home for Mum.

'Now just a minute,' he said. 'Tell me, did I get this right? Did I actually hear you say you wanted me to steal army rations for you to take home?'

'No, I didn't say that at all. It's like this, since I won't be having another meal in camp for the remainder of the week. I thought you might like to let me have part of the unexpired portion of my week's rations.'

'Well, well! I can't believe I'm hearing this. Would you care to elaborate a little and tell me just what you had in mind?'

'Look, don't bother,' I sighed. 'It's just that I didn't want to be a burden on my family. The food situation isn't real good at home, as you well know.'

'You'd better get yourself out of here before I put your name on a 252 – a charge sheet – there's nothing doing.'

After this little setback, something I hadn't really contemplated, there was just enough time for me to pick up my respirator from the tent before making my way down to get the bus. As I strolled down near the cookhouse I noticed the corporal cook standing there. He was making some kind of gesture, with his head turning and cocked to one side.

Looking behind me and seeing no one that could be the subject of his attention, I began to think that maybe he'd decided to put my name on a charge sheet after all. He continued to stare at me and this was enough to make me go over and ask what he wanted, before getting a pleasant surprise as it seemed he'd had a change of heart.

After making sure the coast was clear, he invited me to join him in the cookhouse storeroom, where he told me to stuff a tin of pink salmon and a tin of bully beef into my respirator haversack.

'I never gave you that,' he said. 'Off you go!'

We left Salisbury just after 5.30 p.m., and by 6.30 p.m. my thoughts were all on Birmingham and my family. As I sat in the dimly lit bus, I found myself working out a program that would pack as much as possible into the next forty-eight hours.

We stopped briefly at a country pub on the main road near Banbury, and about an hour later the driver told us that we would probably arrive in Brum about nine-thirty, and that he proposed to drop us on one of the side streets in the vicinity of New Street Station and would pick us up at the same place at half-past four on Sunday afternoon.

The journey was a bit drawn out. I hadn't travelled by road during the blackout before and most of the time hadn't the faintest idea where we were. Then, around nine o'clock, we saw searchlights swinging their beams in a wide arc across the sky towards the north-east, giving the impression they were probably in a training session.

The bus hadn't gone much further before we had to revise that assumption because ack-ack fire could now be seen in the distance. Luckily for us we seemed to be moving further away from it. The bus appeared to be running pretty much to schedule as we began to slow down in traffic approaching Birmingham from the south-east.

Suddenly the whole area ahead came to life.

'It seems we've arrived at the same time as the Luftwaffe!' the driver shouted, keeping his head down and his eyes on the road, not wanting to lose any time.

As we moved slowly through the outer Birmingham suburbs, he said hurriedly, 'Look, fellows, we'd better make that return trip at 3.30 p.m., not 4.30. Does everyone understand that? I will be leaving right on time. It's to make sure we clear the city in daylight allowing for minor delays.'

There wasn't exactly panic, but no one wasted any time getting off the bus. Our arrival a few hundred yards from Station Street coincided with some heavy gun fire, and as a cone of searchlights beamed almost directly overhead I was regretfully reminded that I'd left my steel helmet back in the tent.

The rest of the fellows and the bus disappeared in seconds, leaving me standing there alone and a little bewildered. We'd been dropped in a part of town that I wasn't familiar with, while flashes of gun fire and an overpowering amount of noise helped to make the situation even more confusing.

After walking around for a moment or two I was able to establish where I was and to further familiarise myself with the location, making sure that I wouldn't have any difficulty finding the place where we were going to be picked up for the return journey.

And so, it wasn't long before my hobnailed boots were echoing at a good infantry pace as I made my way along the cobbledstone surface of Jamaica Row.

Heading off along Bradford Street, I looked over my shoulder a couple of times for a 31A bus and didn't feel too optimistic about the prospects of one showing up. Most of the few vehicles that were on the move were fire tenders and ambulances. Anti-aircraft fire was so intense I had to seek cover just after leaving Bradford Street, near Camp Hill.

I was wishing I'd brought along my steel helmet. While sheltering, lying at the foot of heavy timbered and wrought iron doors just inside the arched entrance to a church, bombs began screaming down, followed by heavy explosions that made the building shake violently.

Soon after heading off again and realising that although I wasn't actually running I'd raised the pace a little, and seemed to have had a whole section of the normally very busy Stratford Road all to myself. Like rabbits sensing danger, the locals too were down in their holes, the near empty streets a weird contrast to what was happening in the sky above.

For the next mile I can remember easily exceeding a light-infantry pace and my hobnails were in unison to the rhythm of "Run, Rabbit, Run". Half an hour later, along Warwick Road near Sparkhill, I was once again forced to take cover, this time in the arcade-style entrance to a large store. While sheltering there I made the acquaintance of a special police constable who'd had the same idea. He told me that Sparkhill had suffered several recent raids and the public had stood up to them well despite some very sad stories. After about twenty minutes or so the raid eased off enough for me to get moving again. I said cheerio to the copper and as he hadn't been able to raise my hopes regarding a bus, got back on shanks's pony.

As I moved down the Warwick Road, I passed the old Tyseley Cinema just as the whole district was lit up by flares. They'd quickly turned night into day drifting slowly in the direction of Small Heath, Eddie Atkinson's stamping ground.

Towards Small Heath came the crunch of several bombs detonating in quick succession, while a closer solitary bomb brought the widespread clatter of breaking glass, caused by the many roofing tiles that had became missiles after being blasted from a building that was hit on an adjacent street.

Guns put up a ferocious barrage. Shrapnel started to rain down, making the most demoralising sounds before rattling rooftops or coming to a crashing halt on bitumen. Rifle fire could be heard mingled with gun fire and seemed to be coming from a side street. The firing must have been directed at flares, but didn't appear to be very successful.

A little further on, as I crouched on steps between brick walls at the entrance to a building that was elevated a few feet above road level, I heard the sounds of laughter. Hardly more than twenty yards away, a boy aged about nine or ten and a little girl maybe a couple of years younger, had raced out into the middle of a road devoid of traffic.

Because the night had suddenly become day, they were holding hands and screaming with laughter as they gazed up at the flares, quite unaware of the danger they were facing from falling shrapnel. The boy shouted out that they'd better get going and they dashed away, still holding hands, disappearing into a house on the far side of the road.

As darkness gradually returned to the Warwick Road, I thought I heard the distant sound of a bus. Moving sharply to the other side of the road with my fingers crossed, hoping that at last my luck may have changed, the sound was definitely getting closer.

Suddenly, out of the darkness appeared not one bus but at least four or five of them. I half-heartedly edged away from the kerb in the hope that I might be picked up, but it wasn't to be. These buses were most likely making their way from the more vulnerable city garages, to safer dispersal areas in the outer suburbs and weren't allowed to stop.

It must have been close to midnight. The number of hold-ups since leaving the city centre had more than doubled the time I'd expected to get home. Fires were raging in several directions; the worst seemed to be towards the suburbs of Small Heath and Bordesley. German aircraft continued to drone above, and while they were still getting the full attention of searchlights, gun fire seemed to be more sporadic.

While moving through Tyseley near Wharfdale Road, I was hailed by two women who were standing at the side of Warwick Road near the intersection. They seemed a little distressed, but, although fires were raging close by, illuminating the area near where they stood, they didn't appear to be too worried about the raid and crossed the road to speak to me. The elder of the two, a woman about forty, looked me over in a kind of parental manner before asking where I was heading. When I told them Acock's Green, she asked if I would mind if the younger one accompanied me as far as Olton, and I cautiously agreed.

We moved away from the glow of burning buildings, and, after walking for a couple of minutes, I learned from the young woman that she'd just left her job at the Rover factory to go home so that she could take care of her mother. She told me she held fears for her ailing mother who was at home by herself, and that her father was an Auxiliary Fireman and hardly ever got home because of the continual raids.

From our conversation I learned she was a capstan-lathe operator engaged in important war work, but when bombs began shaking the building she was unable to concentrate on her work, fearing for her mother's wellbeing. There wasn't any need for her to tell me she came from Wales, even though her delightful accent was almost constantly being interrupted by gun fire.

She told me the other woman was the duty nurse that had accompanied her from the factory to Warwick Road, hoping to get her on a bus. This young lady hadn't appeared to be at all scared of the raid; she'd obviously had a lot more experience of raids than me, and I remember trying my hardest not to let on that I was feeling a lot less comfortable about the situation.

The best part of an hour after gaining a very pleasant walking companion we passed the Dolphin pub, and it was as we approached the Lincoln Road intersection that a large bomb seemed to detonate extremely close by.

Then, while she was speaking, the drone of approaching German raiders was interrupted by the scream of more bombs, this time close enough for us to have to dive for cover. The young woman quickly dragged herself alongside me as we lay on pavement at the foot of a masonry wall, eventually squeezing closely between me and the wall while anticipating a number of bomb blasts.

As we lay there snugly, a strong smell of cutting oil from her work clothes had me reminiscing the times I'd walked through machine shops at Webley and Scott's. Those days now seemed a lifetime away. She'd obviously left work in a hurry and not had time to change out of her work clothes or put on a face – not that she needed to have worried too much about the latter, I thought. We got back on our feet and decided to move on.

At the Lincoln Road intersection a few minutes later, I told her we would now have to part company and go our respective ways.

'I have a mother, too,' I told her. She replied that she'd been hoping that I could have made it to her home and that it wouldn't be too far out of my way. I was explaining to her that I'd already walked from the city centre and that time was very precious for me. But then, the sound of enemy bombers began attracting a lot more gun fire, suggesting the raid was starting to hot up again and I found myself heading off in the direction of her home. It must have been her way of expressing her gratitude when she gently slipped her arm under mine a few moments later.

After walking a few more minutes, we stood mid-span on the bridge that crossed the Grand Union Canal. We turned and looked towards the City. The glow from so many fires was absolutely breathtaking.

'That's where I live,' she said, pointing in the direction of Pierce Avenue. 'It's on the high ground about half a mile away.'

'You'll be all right now, won't you?' I asked, before telling her that I had to go. She looked a little more at ease as she turned towards me, gently dumping her dilly-bag on the pavement before standing directly in front of me and softly sliding her fingers beneath my shoulder epaulets, glow from fires and searchlights reflecting on her face and glossy dark hair effectively causing her eyes to glisten.

It's gotta be the Brylcreem, I silently said to myself, guessing she was about to give me the pleasure of another unexpected opportunity to bury my face into her factory attire. It was only then that I realised what beautiful features she had. She gave me what felt like a very slow motherly kiss on the cheek as she hugged me tightly, thanking me and telling me she thought she would be all right, now that she'd got past the canal.

As she turned to go, she said, 'You're not that old, are you?'

Our smiles turned to laughter. I then stood there feeling a little sorrowful as I watched her slowly move downhill before disappearing into the night. It would have given me a nice feeling to have seen her cast a casual glance back, but she didn't. I understood. There was only one person on her mind and soon she would be home comforting her. She'd told me her family came from the town of Neath in South Wales and it was the war that had brought them to Birmingham. She thought her parents might decide to stay in Brum and said she very much hoped they would.

There have been many times since that I've thought about that ship that passed in the night. I've also wondered if she'd had any real inkling that the "stormtrooper" of close on two months, who had provided her escort during the raid was actually a fourteen-year-old. I was still thinking about her and her particular kind of nicety as I turned and made my way in the opposite direction towards my home. Funny, but we hadn't even bothered to ask each other's names. This kind of thing must only happen in wartime, I thought. What a pity we hadn't had more time; she might even have taken me to the pictures.

In less than half an hour I was once again walking the street where I lived. Searchlights were providing just sufficient light to silhouette two more recently bombed houses that were quite close to my home. One of them had been the home of Fred Bennett who was another of my school classmates. Poor old Mum must have walked past these bomb sites each day but made no mention of them in her latest letter. I can remember thinking she must now be following Churchill's example of suppressing unfavourable information.

The raid showed no signs of abating. Not long after 1 a.m. I was knocking on the front door of my home. I was tired. There was no response. Of course, how stupid of me – they'll be in the shelter. Within a minute I was lifting up the potato sack and gazing down into the cold bleak candlelight of Britain's last line of defence. My mother and younger brother Larry got quite a shock.

Chapter Four: A Surprise Visitor in Khaki

Mum and Larry had never had a visitor to the shelter during an air raid before, but soon worked out this unexpected intruder in uniform wasn't one of those German paratroopers that thousands of posters had warned the public to be alert for since the invasion threat began in June.

Gazing up out of candlelight they'd understandably been a little shocked at first, but quickly recognised me though they were seeing me in khaki for the first time. After exchanging a few words, my mother wasn't able to restrain her anxiety any longer, pleading with me to go to the house and persuade my brother John to join us in the shelter as the raid was proving to be one of the worst they'd had.

My sixteen-year-old brother John was sound asleep when I entered his bedroom and too tired to show any emotions on seeing me. After I'd passed on Mum's urgent request, he gave a sort of restrained smile.

'Tell her I'm too tired,' he said.

My mother wasn't a bit surprised. John was dedicated to working long hours at the Castle Bromwich aircraft factory, travelling back and forth on his motorcycle each day and not always in ideal conditions. He also devoted most of his limited leisure time to the Local Defence Volunteers, later to become the Home Guard, as he awaited his call-up for the RAF.

By 4 a.m., we were having a cup of tea in the house, but my mother remained on tenterhooks until dawn, as we played out what must have been a regular routine for hundreds of thousands of Britain's city dwellers during those long cold nights of late 1940. Larry told me he would be joining his schoolmates in rural Wales the following week and was now looking forward to the venture. 'I'd like to be taking Mum with me,' he said. 'Mum's the one who really needs the break. This war's putting years on her, she must be really missing Dad.' This from my twelve-year old brother!

For the next four hours, I slept. My old bed had never felt so good, I then sat half awake, gazing down over our back-yard air raid shelter. The day was typically cold and dull, as was the gloom that came with the BBC news. Birmingham's raid hadn't even rated a mention next to London's woes, making our problems in Brum appear minor compared with those down south. Poor devils, I thought. Cripes! How bad must it be in London?

My mother managed to give me a nice breakfast around ten o'clock but John was still in bed. She was thrilled with the couple of tins of food I'd brought from camp; she knew that I must have been thinking about them.

'We'll have that after you've gone back,' she said. 'And Joe, your Dad told me in a letter last week he's no longer in the Warwicks, and there's a rumour his next move will be to somewhere a bit warmer.'

It would want to be, Dad had written, 'This place is so windy and cold and needless to say there's nothing in the way of entertainment.'

'Why haven't they fixed the water problem in the shelter?' I asked Mum. 'Haven't you any idea when it'll be done?'

'Don't worry, they'll be taking care of it very soon,' she told me. 'The contractors are only a few houses down the road now. One of them called in to look at the shelter on Wednesday. He must have been the foreman and I think he was an Irishman; he had a strong accent. After I'd made him a cup of tea, he promised me he'd have it fixed within a fortnight at the most.'

'Look, Joe, there is something that I wasn't going to tell you, but perhaps it's as well if you know now. It's about Mrs Savins. Do you remember when the Savins got an option to move to another house some months ago, and they'd decided to take it?'

This was because Mr Savins worked night shifts. The house offered was considered to be in a safer area than here and this suited Mrs Savins who had to spend most nights alone with her very young children.

My mother was trying hard to fight back tears when she told me, 'Something really terrible had happened. Following an air raid alert Mrs Savins went through her regular routine of putting the children in a little cubby they'd made for them under the stairs, hoping they'd be safe there. But, during the raid a bomb exploded quite close alongside their home, she was injured and survived, but the three kiddies were killed.'

Unfortunately, falling bombs didn't recognise innocents, they were so young they didn't stand a chance. Until a few months ago the Savins had been living in a semi-detached home in the same block as ours.

Mrs Savins was my mother's only close friend and although Mum was pleased for them, I knew she'd felt a little disappointed when they'd moved further up the road.

David was the eldest of the Savins children, and was often referred to by our family as the "go-between", delighting in carrying regular messages from his mother to mine. He was five years old and an exceptionally good looking and intelligent little boy with a lovely nature, his blue eyes and blond curly hair set off his rosy cheeks and gave him a kind of perpetual smile. He would often spend time at our house being spoiled by my mother. I was really saddened by this news.

Of all the shocking things we'd had to learn to live with in recent months, this must surely be as cruel as it could get. David had been living for the day he would get his big chance to join us older kids playing football in the park. He'd told me he was counting on me to take him there when he got a bit bigger. Remembering this, I'd realised why Mum had thought twice before breaking this horrible news to me.

Before lunch, I decided to put on some warm clothes and took a stroll across the park where I expected to find some of my mates kicking a ball around. The short walk took me across grass that was mantled with heavy dew, beneath trees that were stripped of their leaves. There was a cold light northerly breeze that not only brought a tingle to the tip of my nose but also rendered a silent reminder that these blinking Germans were denying me a precious football season.

A cloud of oily black smoke that hung across the city was drifting slowly in our direction, but other than that, nothing to suggest we were at war. Then, as I turned to make my way back towards home, a number of barrage balloons began rising in the direction of Solihull and Sheldon.

'Don't tell me we're about to get a raid at this time of day!' I said.

I knew there had been daylight raids on several aircraft factories around Birmingham and knew there were Rover "shadow" factories a couple of miles away in that direction.

When I got home my mother was quick to explain about the barrage balloons. 'They're up and down all the time, you know, not necessarily a raid; most likely the girls being put through a training session I expect,' she said.

Later that afternoon, I decided to look up old schoolmates, hoping to catch up on the local scene, telling Mum I'd be home before nine o'clock, sooner if there was a raid. After meeting friends around the Shirley Road area, I strolled down through Acock's Green village, feeling a little disappointed and finding it hard to believe that in just a couple of months the war could have so thoroughly changed the life-styles of even the most ardent of my footballing mates. Sure, they still kicked a ball around; in fact several had even played club football that afternoon. But that's where it all ended. Very few socialised any more.

Now that the raids had become so bad, there was a tendency to avoid places such as cinemas and the local dances. There had been a direct hit on a cinema not far from here just a couple of nights ago I was told, leaving at least twenty dead. On the other hand, pubs had remained much the same and were still very popular – so many people wanting to mask their sorrows, no doubt.

Before heading home, I managed to bump into Jimmy Jackson, one of my old schoolmates. Jimmy was one of the few still carrying on regardless, his defiance made me laugh. He'd have you believing Hitler was nothing more than another character out of a comic strip, and was determined not to let the war interfere with his hobnobbing.

Like me, Jimmy was fourteen, and had been my classmate and a very good friend for the past three years. I remember sitting with him that evening in Fred's Cafe in Acock's Green village, drinking tea as we listened to the day's football results coming through the radio. Jimmy told me how surprised he'd been to see me in khaki and how much he would like to have been in the navy. He couldn't wait for the navy to accept him as soon as he turned sixteen.

When I told him he could get into the army right away, he told me he didn't want to be a footslogger and was prepared to sit it out until the navy sent for him. He was a smart, good-looking lad and although he wouldn't have been much above five-foot-seven he seemed to attract more than his fair share of the opposite sex. I imagined they'd have found him irresistible in bell-bottoms. He was also a very intelligent lad who always did well at school; his exam results were often the envy of the rest of the class.

Back home I had a cup of tea and a sandwich with Mum, and we discussed the big question: would the bombers turn up that night? It was already after nine o'clock and flying conditions looked good, but no alert had sounded.

'You know, Joe, we don't need air raid sirens around here,' my mother said. 'The dogs always bark when there's going to be a raid, often long before the sirens sound. It's true, isn't it John?'

'You're so right, Mum. It really doesn't take much to make the blinking dogs howl around here. What do you think Dad meant when he said he'd heard his next move would be to somewhere a little warmer?'

'Well, I really don't know, I believe it must be so inhospitable where he is at this time of the year, just about anywhere else would be warmer.'

I suggested to Mum that he might be going to Egypt now that the Italians had entered the war.

On Sunday morning, I was unable to resist the temptation to have a traditional kick-around with the lads in the park, knowing it would be the last for a while. It seemed great to be getting back into football togs, even though I got to hear the sad story about Westfield, my former club, and its dismal performance so far that season. I also felt a little guilty when I heard Westfield were only able to field ten players for two of their games.

One of my close friends, Fred "Busty" Dolphin, who played for Woodlands told me he'd missed out on a game that Saturday because a bomb had exploded smack on the centre spot of the pitch they were to have played. He said it was a big bomb and they would need a bulldozer to level the field out again. If it hadn't happened during a night raid he told me, he'd have sworn the bloody Jerries had done it deliberately.

Before two o'clock that afternoon, my hobnails were noisily pounding the stairs of a council bus that was heading for the city. I found leaving home that Sunday much harder than the last time I'd said goodbye to Mum. Now that the air raids were so much worse than anyone could have predicted, I questioned whether joining the army had been the right thing to do.

Arriving early near Station Street gave me enough time to take a short stroll over to look at the legendry Bull Ring, the place where hordes of Midlanders flocked to the markets.

A visit to the Bull Ring for a lot of Brummies wasn't just another spending spree, but a chance to participate in a tradition that had gone on there for many generations. Our occasional family jaunts ceased when Dad went away in the army and we'd heard recent air raids had taken their toll, bombs and fires devastating much of the area around the market place. Before the war and Birmingham's introduction to the Blitz, it was possible for shoppers to buy just about anything at the Bull Ring in an atmosphere and language peculiar only to the Midlands.

Shoppers and visitors alike breezed around the markets each day, some only bargain hunting, others happy to stand back quietly while watching the antics and listening to the humour of traders, especially the banter that was forever present along the rows of keenly competitive barrow boys.

Sadly much had changed. I found it hard to visualise any form of gaiety flourishing from around the market area that afternoon, making it difficult for me to recapture any image of our family's pre-war visits. They'd been the days that for Dad, Mum and my brothers were always fun days, enjoyed with an air of laughter that went arm in arm with outbursts of spontaneous off-the-cuff humour, the merriment always complemented by an aroma of roasting chestnuts and baked potatoes along with street entertainers of all kinds.

Many large buildings had been flattened and spread across an area predominantly that of the barrow boys, while others were minus their roofs. Fire blackened walls of gutted stores bore testimony that the Luftwaffe had done its job around the market place all right.

Where would Dad be able to buy us crabs and whelks now, and where else would he be able to get us jellied eels?

I stood on the pavement near the bottom steps of the smoke-blackened fish market for a moment or two while trying to re-live happier days there with the rest of the family. But when I felt my eyes becoming moist I thought I'd better move on; you're a soldier now, I had to quickly remind myself.

As I sadly made my way over to get the bus, I had the feeling it was going to be a long, long time before that little chip of "Merry England" would return to grace the Bull Ring again.

The bus left just after 3.30 p.m. with no absentees. For me, it was back to the army again. The dwindling daylight hours were spent crossing Oxfordshire, where my father and many generations of his farming family originated. I'd often wondered what made Dad break away from family traditions to start a new life in the industrial

Midlands. My brothers and I thought it must have been something very special, because he'd retained a great love of the land. His knowledge of farming and the rural way of life in general came to the fore during the Depression years. Unlike most others who dwelt in the less affluent suburbs around Birmingham, thanks to Dad, our family was hardly affected by the Depression. We were never without home grown fruit and vegetables.

Similarly, our inability to afford most cuts of meat went unnoticed; Dad maintaining a fairly regular supply of rabbits and game. Pigeon pie was on the table as often as once a week when things did get a bit tough and not all the birds were of the woodland variety. Some had actually clocked good times from places as far away as France and Spain, their sacrifice made a little less painful for Dad by my mother's cooking expertise.

Stepping off the bus back at camp gave me the feeling I'd only been away a couple of hours. Maybe the army was having a bigger influence on me than I realised. Light rain was beginning to sweep across the camp as I slipped quietly into the tent, and to the sound of raindrops gently tapping away at the canvas a few inches above my head, I curled up under the blankets and slept till Reveille.

Walking down the tent line for breakfast I noticed a small group had gathered, their eyes fixed on the main entrance at the top end of the camp, where Regimental Sergeant Major Geard accompanied the camp commander on what appeared to be an inspection of deteriorating conditions following more rain.

By chance, on entering the mess tent, the first person I should front was the corporal cook.

'Oh! So you got back alright then,' he remarked as he heaped mashed potatoes onto my plate, mash being part of one of his limited culinary lines.

Served with a couple of sausages and thick onion gravy, it was commonly referred to in camp as "zeppelins in the fog", arguably one of his tastier meals and was well received by most of the chaps. We'd already learned the cook's presence in the mess tent generally indicated the meal was one of his better offerings.

On occasions when his concoctions failed expectations, he appeared less sociable, choosing to lie low. All in all, he wasn't too bad a bloke really. And, for a chap who little more than twelve months earlier had been fully employed selling newspapers near one of Birmingham's main railway stations, you'd have to say he was unassumingly doing his share towards the war effort. Aside from that, I knew his heart was in the right place.

'Yes, and thanks again, Corporal, you made my mother very happy,' I told him. His plain and slightly occupationally weathered face remained dead-pan.

Inclement weather had restricted some of our training to lectures, but we had one group in camp that refused to let the rain interfere with their training program. They were the buglers, under the guidance of a regular soldier, the very popular Corporal Lane. Each day, regardless of weather conditions, they'd occupy a spot near a spinney on the east side of a small hill a little more than half a mile from camp. There were only four of them, but their distant bugle calls echoed out constantly, and their improvement quite noticeable.

On that Monday afternoon I caught up with Eddie Atkinson who was pleased to see me, knowing I'd just got back from his side of Brum. I was very careful not to let on that I thought the suburb of Small Heath had been copping it. Instead, I told him the bombing had seemed to be fairly widespread and, also how long it had taken for me to finally get home following my much-interrupted walk from the city centre.

'Yeah, someone else told me the raids were getting worse. I might try to get home myself soon to see how my old man's coping.'

'What happened here over the weekend?' I asked.

'Oh, yes,' he said. 'There is one interesting news item. The YMCA canteen will no longer accept a cash deposit for a knife and fork. They have some other arrangement now. I think you have to leave your hat and get it back with a cloakroom ticket.'

'Well, it sounds like a good idea. I know someone

who'll be more than pleased to hear that.'

The return of the British Expeditionary Force from Dunkirk had created a major accommodation problem in June, 1940, and that situation still existed. We were told that under normal circumstances, camps like ours that showed signs of becoming waterlogged would have to be evacuated. But, for tens of thousands of servicemen in our predicament, there just wasn't any under-roof accommodation available. The conditions at the cricket ground worsened on Sunday morning, and by the afternoon a most extraordinary state of affairs had developed.

An unwritten law in the British Army, especially within infantry battalions, was effective during off-duty periods, mainly weekend afternoons. On those occasions an "in bed or out of barracks" rule applied. Steady rain was falling and few of the men still in camp could have afforded the cost of a packet of Woodbines, so it wasn't surprising that almost all of them were indulging in the only other luxury available, a warm bed.

Then, very uncharacteristically for a Sunday afternoon, came a bugle call for the men to fall in at the double. 'What the hell's going on?' was the immediate reaction. And in most tents there was little or no move to find out. The call was repeated, this time followed by Reveille, also at the double and it was after this second call that we agreed, in our tent anyway, that the bugler must have been getting into the grog, and we didn't even bother to open the tent flap.

We then heard loud voices from adjacent tents; someone was shouting for us to get out. I took a peep over towards the guard tent and saw Regimental Sergeant Major Geard standing beside the bugler, who was still calling the men to fall in.

The rain continued to bucket down. Corporals and sergeants walked the lines telling everyone they had to carry what gear they could and form up in three ranks close to the tent line. Apparently, RSM Geard, without the authorisation of a commissioned officer, had decided to abandon the camp after finding men were no longer able to prevent a constant stream of surface water running through their tents, satisfying himself that the situation now presented a health risk. The scene was pretty dismal: nearly three hundred men all overloaded with gear and only their ground sheets to keep off the rain, were lined up in a quagmire awaiting RSM Geard to indicate the next move.

The strategy the sergeant major had worked out was dependent on the hospitality of local civilians. He'd planned to door-knock along two roads heading towards Salisbury begging people to take in a soldier, two if possible, to relieve a temporary emergency. The column that I found myself in left the camp at the lower gate moving slowly while sergeants did the door knocking.

The response was far better than we'd expected. Salisbury was a garrison town that had been host to many more than the average number of service personnel, and you'd have thought the civilian population of Salisbury would have become sick of the sight of men in uniform since the outbreak of war. But after travelling about half a mile or so there were only sixty men to find accommodation for. Out of the blue we halted in front of a private club on the southern side of the road, and the rest of us were pleasantly put up there.

The RSM's initiative was not received too lightly by the camp commander who was a major, and he wasted little time letting his feelings be known.

The following day, a hastily convened court found Regimental Sergeant Major Geard had over-stepped his authority when evacuating the camp, and was subsequently demoted to the rank of sergeant. The very popular Geard may have been lowered in rank, but in the eyes of most of us he'd been elevated higher in our esteem. That afternoon, we were able to return to our tents to collect any possessions we'd left behind. It then became apparent that stumps had finally been drawn on the Wiltshire County Cricket Ground as far as the Dorsetshire Regiment was concerned. Two days later, a convoy of troop carriers arrived and within minutes we were on our way to Chippenham, a move that didn't take long for us to realise was just another stop-gap arrangement.

My company occupied a small school on the outskirts of Chippenham, and we stayed there for a couple of weeks. The school was near a railway freight depot and adjacent to a trucking complex garaging large milk tankers. We had hot milk each evening. Chippenham proved to be a popular town for the Dorsets, most of our accommodation being within easy walking distance of the town centre.

The weather was also a little friendlier, making it possible to help catch up on our delayed training program. On pay parade a couple of days later, our quartermaster raised a smile when he told me he had good news: the missing greatcoat was now paid for in full. So, as from the following Friday, instead of the proverbial "king's shilling" that I'd been receiving for the past eight weeks, I'd soon be getting a king's ransom: all of nine shillings.

The following week during rifle drill, our attention was drawn to a light aircraft that seemed to be in difficulties just a few hundred yards away. Our sergeant drill instructor got a bit hot under the collar when he lost the squad's attention, not realising what was happening behind his back.

The aircraft, a Tiger Moth, began to nose dive towards the ground from just a few hundred feet, the sergeant turning in time to see its final plunge into a grassy meadow close by.

'Let's go!' he shouted, and the squad took off across the school sports field in haste.

We were at the scene within a minute, but found the pilot had died on impact. His head could be seen alongside the aircraft's engine that had burrowed several feet into soft earth. We remained at the site until members of the RAF arrived.

The next payday came, and, although it was to be the big one for me, my pay would remain in my pocket for at least another twenty-four hours because I'd been listed for guard duties. Our temporary guardroom at Chippenham was the school sports pavilion, located seventy or eighty yards from classrooms, which were being used as sleeping quarters for about a hundred men.

The pavilion had two rooms and stood on piers about four or five feet above natural ground level. Entry was by a flight of timbered steps about four feet wide. Lance Corporal Baylis was the guard commander on what turned out for me to be a most unusual night, a night I'm never likely to forget.

In our unit it was normal for Friday nights to be quiet. As soon as their duties were finished for the day, most of the chaps couldn't wait to get into town with a few bob to spend. Only the more prudent would be dining in the mess room on Friday nights, and, as with most infantry units, prudence seemed to trail very secondary in our company.

By nine o'clock, two or three men returning from town reported to the guardroom and were recorded as returning to quarters, SPD – Sober and Properly Dressed. Soon after, others followed. One of them, a corporal, told us there'd been a bit of trouble in one of the pubs at the top end of town, but he'd been unable to elaborate any further, other than to say he had seen Dorsets in that pub earlier in the evening.

Hearing another corporal's account just before ten o'clock, a picture started to emerge. We knew then that what started as a discussion over a few drinks had turned into a violent argument, one soldier leaving the pub in a hurry, another threatening to get him.

At ten o'clock, I took up sentry duties at the foot of the guardroom steps and, about half an hour later, I was confronted by Private Joe Hulland returning early from a night on the town. He surprised me by making an unusual request, stating he wished to seek asylum in the guardroom and that he considered his life was in real danger.

After taking a closer look at Hulland, a fellow who hailed from Acock's Green, it was obvious he was in a state of distress, his face also showing signs of a dustup. Corporal Baylis decided he'd better let him get his head down in the guardroom then joined me a few minutes later, telling me that under no circumstances was I to allow Jack Pettit access to the guardroom if he still appeared to be troublesome.

'That could be a tall order,' I told him.

Pettit, a South African in his mid-twenties, and of huge physique, was a lovely, very well-liked chap when sober, but had also been known to become a raving madman following one of his occasional heavy drinking sprees.

'Look, Joe,' said the corporal, 'with a bit of luck, he won't find out we have Hulland here in the guardroom.'

'Yeah,' I replied glumly, 'and if he does, I hope it's after midnight when someone else is on Stag.'

'Don't worry,' he said. 'If you have any trouble with him, just turn out the guard. OK?'

He went back into the guardroom, closing the door behind him. It suddenly became dark, cold and quiet. It must have been around eleven o'clock. Another hour and I'll have my head down, I was thinking.

Two more chaps checking in at the guardroom around 11.20 p.m. claimed to have seen Pettit about an hour earlier at a dance, where he'd made a brief appearance. They were under the impression that he must have been looking for a particular woman. I began to think that perhaps my luck was holding and that Pettit's interest in the guardroom's occupant might have waned.

All hopes of an uneventful night faded as the unmistakable hulk of Jack Pettit moved stubbornly past the guardroom on his way to the sleeping quarters, obstinately disregarding his commitment to report in on his return to the billets.

Then almost immediately I heard the sound of timber breaking and men shouting. Then more sounds of timber being smashed, as some lights in the sleeping quarters were switched on. There appeared to be no let-up as the uproar continued. There'd been no need for me to call out the guard. Corporal Baylis and the rest of the guard were already standing on the veranda above the steps. Company Quartermaster Wilson then came running towards the guardroom, waving his arms with rage, and yelling for the guard commander.

'You've got to stop him,' he shouted. 'He's already smashed his way through five internal doors and if he gets Joe Hulland he said he'll kill him.'

I looked up at the guard commander before deciding to move on to the second of the steps, knowing how tall Pettit was. About half a minute later, Pettit appeared out of the darkness with a dozen or so of the fellows following not far behind, none of them wanting to miss out on the David and Goliath spectacle they thought was about to unfold.

'Have you got him in there?' Pettit growled, as he got within fifteen feet of the steps.

For me, the moment of reckoning had arrived. I immediately adopted the "on-guard" position, with my bayonet pointing directly towards Jack's chest, causing a brief moment of silence as the onlookers awaited the next move. This came when Pettit reached out with his right hand and managed to grab the safety rail of the steps.

The CQM, who was now standing about twenty feet away, called out to me, 'Give him the bayonet! Don't let him get on the steps – do you hear what I'm saying?'

I heard what he was saying all right, but I couldn't believe he was saying it. My bayonet was now almost pressing against Jack's tunic in the region of his heart, but this didn't stop him from exerting pressure as he tried to use the hand rail to pull himself onto the steps. Once more the QM urged me to use the bayonet on the tall South African.

It was then that Pettit looked me in the eyes and said, 'You wouldn't do that to me, would you? Just let me get in there.'

I felt flabbergasted because my bayonet, now only inches from his throat, was having no apparent effect on his determination. The staff sergeant continued to scream at me, saying that he'd have me charged if I didn't obey his order.

I realised the situation had escalated into something even more ticklish than I'd first anticipated. Quite apart from the fact that I was scared, I felt an obligation to keep the big fellow off the steps. Even though it was a cold night, perspiration was running across my forehead and into my eyes, making it difficult for me to see clearly. I clasped my rifle for dear life as there was nothing that

I could do about it. I decided to edge myself slightly backwards to gain the height of one more step and as I did so, a split-second lapse in my concentration must have allowed Pettit to grab the stock of my rifle with his left hand. This move caused him to slightly lose his balance momentarily, allowing me to seize the opportunity to apply downward pressure across his chest, enabling me to use the weight of my rifle to further off-balance him and cause him to stumble backwards.

The entourage of onlookers, along with the rest of the guard, were then able to quickly take advantage of the right moment to subdue Pettit, holding him at the foot of the steps until he could be restrained. Thus ending what must have been a nightmare for Joe Hulland.

Many times I've thought about this incident and, the probability of it being unique in the annals of the British Army, a staff sergeant actually ordering a soldier to bayonet a member of his own unit under those circumstances was quite remarkable.

Of all the incidents that I got involved in as a fourteen-year-old, this one was among those that were engraved deepest in my memory. When I'd held the bayonet at Jack's throat, as far as I was concerned, it was an attempt to call his bluff. But this was just wishful thinking on my part and a measure of my youthful inexperience. He was so drunk and angry that he was devoid of any power of reasoning.

Staff Sergeant Wilson, who was no youngster, probably regretted ever ordering me to take such violent action. On Saturday morning I think he'd begun to realise he'd over-reacted to the situation. He must have really thought he was saving Hulland's life. He now looked a very tired man, showing signs of someone urgently in need of help, and in only a matter of days was transferred away from our unit.

Some credit should have been given to the guard commander, who was always close at hand during the confrontation. He seemed to have had a very good understanding of what the circumstances required, and was able to keep his head, knowing that an intemperate intervention by a third party could well have resulted in bloodshed.

This incident ended what had otherwise been a pleasant stay for me and the rest of the Dorsets at Chippenham. The battalion moved to nearby Corsham a week or so later.

Within a week of our arrival at Corsham, we feasted on a hastily prepared and very austere Christmas dinner, while occupying dormitory type quarters that were still under construction, and situated close to the perimeter of the beautiful estate of an Edwardian manor. We then learned to everyone's surprise that we'd got to move quickly to prepare for our first official defence duties.

The following day we boarded a troop train on what turned out to be a long drawn-out tour of southern England. We hadn't the slightest idea of our destination when the train headed north. There were plenty of speculations. Rumours suggesting we were on our way to Liverpool to get a boat caused a bit of wild talk, but was soon discounted as we hadn't been issued with tropical gear. Aside from that, we'd completed little more than half of our basic training.

At times, the train moved only at walking pace, which did nothing to ward off the boredom we were feeling after a few hours within the crowded carriages. A laugh was raised when two chaps left the train to stretch their legs, walking alongside the slowly moving carriages. They came close to being left behind somewhere in the heart of Camelot country when the locomotive suddenly began gaining momentum and they'd had to be dragged hastily back on board.

Another fellow, a chap by the name of Philips, actually fired his rifle from a carriage window into the green hills of Somerset, an offence that would have earned him at least twenty-eight days field punishment had he been caught. Philips was a bit of a loner, who hailed from Aston, and pridefully considered himself as coming from the cultural centre of Birmingham. I hadn't had a lot to do with him, and from what little conversation we'd had, my feelings were that joining the army may well have given Philips his first real opportunity to put the "cultural centre" behind him.

After nearly five hours, we were given haversack rations on a side track just out from Bristol before heading off once more, the train driver still performing as though trying to kill time. The general feeling at this stage was that the delays were most likely brought about by enemy air attacks in the vicinity of our destination. By late afternoon, however, our journey seemed to have become a little more purposeful: we could detect a slight increase in the tempo of the locomotion. Could it be the driver had finally found his way at last?

Just on dark, Company Sergeant Major Trusler made a quick tour of the carriages. He told us he had no idea when or where we would be leaving the train, which, since dark had been moving in a south-easterly direction and around nine o'clock had passed through Eastleigh.

The sergeant major, who was a regular soldier, was able to raise a smile when someone in our compartment worked up enough courage to ask him if he thought perhaps the line may have been bombed. The CSM, like most sergeant majors, was never stuck for words.

His reply came back quick and to the point: 'Good God, man, how the hell would I know? Anything's possible in these times – you shouldn't have to ask me that. And by the way you blokes, just remember you're all getting paid twenty-four hours a day while you're in the army. You don't have to be in a hurry to get anywhere.'

A little later the train was back to walking pace, allowing someone to identify a small creek as being tidal, indicating we had to be closing with the coast again. Then someone pointed out the familiar red glows that we'd learned to associate with towns on fire, causing reflections in the sky in two different directions.

About five or ten miles ahead, there were also searchlights accompanied by ack-ack fire. Still at a walking pace, and while many of the men were asleep, the troop train finally rolled very slowly into Fareham Station around eleven o'clock. Sergeants and officers moved quickly through the carriages urging men to smarten it up a bit, telling us it was important for us to clear the station without wasting too much time.

An air raid was in progress and there was a lot of gun fire. There were also many fires around, one of them close enough to provide a little lighting along platforms. As we raced towards awaiting trucks, it seemed that one of the fires was in the roof of the fire station just across the road. I can vaguely remember seeing fire bombs about to set fire to its roof.

A couple of civilians stood close by gazing up at the roof, but lacking equipment, unable to do anything about the incendiaries. The fire crews, it seemed, must have been away fighting fires in other parts of the town. Everything was happening so quickly. But, even allowing for the air raid, there appeared to be better organisation once we'd left the train.

We were soon on our way again, this time in troop carriers that were painted grey and bore the insignia of the Royal Navy. Half an hour later we arrived at our new place of abode, Lee-on-the-Solent, the closest I'd ever been to the English coastline and a real chance for my first glimpse of the sea.

Chapter Five: Luftwaffe Night Moves

There seemed to be something unusual about the location of our new billet, but, because of the noise and flurry of the air raid on our arrival, I had to wait until daybreak to find out what it was. Most of my platoon had been off-loaded from troop carriers around midnight, taking up residence in a vacant two-storey unfurnished house, which was to become home for about twenty of us in the coming months.

An advance party from the regiment had checked out our new billet days before, placing blankets and paillasses where we were to sleep. No lights could be switched on because windows weren't blacked-out and enemy bombers still occupied nearby air space. However, the reflection from searchlights provided soft lighting in most rooms and we quickly had our beds down. Soon our new home was silent except for the occasional snore.

Loud talking and laughter broke my slumber about an hour before daybreak. I opened my eyes to see Eddie Atkinson raving about our billet being less than a hundred yards from the seafront. He was unable to convince Philips, who made some sordid remarks because he reckoned he was having him on.

As I'd never seen the sea, I dressed quickly and took off up the road. Eddie hadn't been kidding. We were actually residing within a stone's throw of the promenade that overlooked a narrow shingle beach. After gazing out over the choppy water of the Solent in the direction of the Isle of Wight for a minute or two, I can remember feeling a little disappointed. So, this is it then! It's taken me fourteen years, but now with a little assistance from the Fuhrer I've finally made it.

There wasn't a ship in sight. In fact, the scene was so different from the one I'd had locked away in my imagination, looking out over rows of rugged uncompromising barbed wire entanglements, only added to a let-down of my expectations. I wondered what the next surprise would be as I dashed back to make the seven-thirty breakfast parade. We marched in platoon strength to a naval barracks, *HMS Daedalus*, about five minutes away. I didn't have to wait long for the next surprise – the quality of the breakfast served by friendly navy personnel, especially the Wrens who seemed to go out of their way to make sure the Dorsetshires had plenty to eat.

Later in the day, we were lectured on the do's and don'ts of the task we were about to undertake, duties that would come into effect early that evening. We were told we would be guarding the naval air station, primarily in the event of it being used in conjunction with any threatened German invasion attempts.

This, we were told, might come in the form of an enemy airborne force being put down on the airfield. We also had to secure the perimeter of the airfield against any other intruders. Our commanding officer pointed out that the serious invasion threat that had existed over the past three or four months had now been slightly downgraded. He reminded us however that this Fleet Air Arm establishment would still rank high on the enemy's target list. The Germans were well aware that *HMS Daedalus* served as a mothership for the *Ark Royal* as well as a number of other aircraft carriers.

Later that afternoon, my platoon was one of those selected to participate in the takeover of guard duties from men of the Loyal Regiment, a unit that rumour suggested was shortly to be issued with tropical gear. The whole exercise was carried out very quickly, and as a result we weren't given much of a chance to speak to the out-going troops when taking over their pillboxes. And so another milestone was reached – we were about to start earning our two bob a day.

We quickly looked over our allotted pillbox, which contained a Lewis machine gun and several thousand rounds of ammunition. The gun was mounted on a concrete pedestal in the centre of the elevated section of the pillbox, enabling it to be used against aircraft as well as ground targets. In the lower section, the bulk of the ammunition was stored along with enough iron rations to last for a month or so, in the event of the strongpoint becoming isolated in an attack. The Lewis gun was a light machine gun and, as with most weapons used by the British Armed Forces, was of First World War vintage or earlier. It was also designed to be used in the air, not on the ground.

I immediately felt I was looking over a weapon that in its heyday may well have traded shots with Manfred von Richthofen, the "Red Baron". Although a very simple gun, no one in our company had had instructions on this particular type of weapon.

A few hundred yards to our left and right were other machine gun posts the same as ours. That seemed to be the pattern around the whole of the airfield perimeter where dozens of naval aircraft were dispersed about seventy or eighty yards apart. Most of these were old Fairy Swordfish and Albacore biplanes, with the odd Walrus amphibian and a few Roc or Skua dive bombers.

The more recently built hangars at the northern end of the airfield were still intact, but the Luftwaffe had already destroyed sections of the much larger and earlier established hangars situated at the southern end, these had contained the main workshops and administration areas.

The scene there was one of complete devastation, showing remains of several burnt-out aircraft amidst twisted girders that had once supported roofs covering a huge semi-modern complex, parts of which now only blackened walls remained.

Pine aircraft packing cases were positioned at intervals around the eastern side of the airfield and these were used as temporary sleeping quarters for the troops when not doing stints in the gun emplacements. The packing cases were hooked up to what seemed like a shaky Heath Robinson system of coloured lights which, depending on their combinations of colours and intervals of flashing, warned the guard if there was a seaborne or airborne invasion or just another local bombing raid. The latter warning and a few of the others, we were to find out in the coming hours, weren't really necessary.

And so, after eating a good meal, one that had been prepared by the Wrens and sent out to us in the distant parts of the airfield, we sat on the thick concrete parapet of our pillbox and waited. It had been dark for well over an hour. The temperature had fallen enough to make me pull the collar of my greatcoat up around my ears, before impatiently examining the magazine on the gun and gently traversing it 360 degrees with the sights up in the stars.

'Well, you and I are ready, Ken. It's up to Reichsmarschall Goering now.' They were words that didn't mean much, but I can still remember Ken's little sneaky smile. Kenny Baggot was sharing the six till eight stint with me. We were good mates as we both came from Brum and had a few things in common.

But, that first night on the airfield, it was the Luftwaffe that was occupying our thoughts. The fact that less than half-an-hour's flying time was all it took for the Germans to be overhead from their bases in France was sufficient reason to remain alert. You never know, we thought, we may even get a chance to christen the gun.

Just after 7.30 p.m. the corporal of the guard visited our pillbox and told us that supper had arrived. Just as he spoke an alert sounded, prompting him to jump down into the gun pit with us. There was nothing happening around Lee-on-the-Solent, but, in the direction of Portsmouth, searchlights were pointing seawards, their beams probing among sparsely scattered clouds. While Ken and the corporal stood at the gun, I went below and returned with an additional case of magazines.

The scene changed dramatically during the next half hour. The searchlights failed to pick up raiders crossing the airfield. It was almost as if they'd thought the aircraft were our own until bombs began detonating just outside the perimeter, and others about a mile or so away in the direction of Gosport. Before long, a second wave of bombers approached, but this time they were met by a thunderous barrage from guns of all types. When chandelier flares appeared in the sky close by, and while my mates debated what course of action we should take, I was unable to resist the temptation to try out the gun.

The result was very gratifying. On squeezing the trigger, I couldn't believe my eyes when the first of the flares begin to disintegrate, before quickly being snuffed out and a second one going the same way almost immediately. I was sure I'd wasted very little ammo, while the noise from the gun prevented me from hearing any comments that may have been made regarding the appropriateness of my action. This had also created the opportunity for me to be firing my first shots in anger, while still a fourteen-year-old.

Other Dorsets nearby began following our lead, removing the remaining half dozen or so flares from the sky in a matter of minutes, reducing the opportunities for the Germans to select and pin-point targets around the airfield.

We were surprised at the simplicity of our first little encounter with the Luftwaffe, behaving more as if we'd been on the airfield since the war started, rather than just a couple of hours. Then, only a few minutes later, the murderous scream of more bombs sent us on a speedy retreat to the lower section of our pillbox.

I remember two of us laughing like mad after getting jammed tightly in the narrow entrance to the short flight of steps in our haste to get below. The few bombs that were dropped during the raid appeared to have fallen a little wide of the airfield perimeter.

We were learning fast. It had taken just a few hours for us to realise that there was no such thing as two hours on and four hours off. On this assignment we were more likely to be standing at the gun during most hours of darkness. We'd also learned that the gun was very loud for whoever was doing the firing. Ear plugs were a must for this weapon.

The raid was still in progress but centred more towards Portsmouth, where we could see the glow from fires reflecting in the night sky. Later in the evening, the drone of more enemy bombers at high altitude could be heard as they crossed the coast heading north.

Let's hope they're not going to Birmingham were my immediate thoughts, and once again I found myself wondering if the contractors had got around to fixing the water problem in Mum's air raid shelter. Surely they must have done something about it by now.

Around 2 a.m., I managed to get a couple of hours sleep in the packing case, our makeshift guardroom. The rest of the night was uneventful. We actually heard a nightingale as we stood in the gun pit section of our pillbox, this being another first for me.

We never got to hear these beautiful birds near my home. Acock's Green was too built up, I suppose. And yet Vera Lynn had only recently been telling the world she'd sworn she'd heard one sing in Berkeley Square, and every young soldier knew that Vera wouldn't tell a lie. I certainly couldn't imagine anything more peaceful than the pensive performance of this remarkable bird. By chance it had found time to share part of the night with us as we rugged up around the gun, and looked out towards Gosport and the raging fires down that way.

Ken and I watched the dawn break. We could get a better look at the destruction caused during earlier raids on the station, including many bomb craters on and around the airstrip that had only recently been filled. Some of the hits had been remarkably close to our gun pit. In fact, there was very little real estate between a recently filled crater and the position we were occupying. This explained the heavy scarring along the length of the thick concrete parapet of our machine gun post.

As 8 a.m. approached, we looked in the direction of the guardroom expecting to see our relief on the way. Instead we got a visitor from the navy, a chap in his early twenties, in bell-bottoms and carrying a small canvas bag. He introduced himself as the armourer responsible for maintaining the gun and could not hide his frustration when he found it had been fired. He was upset that he'd had to pull cleaning gauze through the barrel, and had the hide to say he thought we'd been wasting ammunition.

This was inviting an early breakdown in army-navy relations, but lucky for him we were too tired to respond.

The new guard arrived shortly after ten o'clock, allowing us to return to our new home by the sea, and the promised twenty-four hours free from all duties. The rest of the guard were quickly under the blankets, but curiosity made me take a hurried stroll to the esplanade again for another quick look at the sea. During this second viewing I noticed the extent of barbed-wire entanglements between the promenade and the narrow shingle beach.

A short distance to the east was a pier that ran a hundred yards or so out into the sea. Some sections had been removed, isolating it from the promenade and from a building with a high tower. Along the seafront nearby were several damaged homes that had already fallen victim of the Luftwaffe, suggesting some German pilots may have released their bombs prematurely in their haste to get back to France.

A few minutes later, I slipped quietly under the blankets, feeling tired but with just a slight sense of satisfaction from firing the gun. Before dropping off I thought these Germans must think they're winning this war.

The way in which they'd so brazenly taken over the sky last night and seeing some of the huge amount of destruction the Luftwaffe had already caused, had given me plenty of food for thought. But knocking those flares out of the sky a few hours earlier, with a type of gun I'd never before set eyes on, enabled me to doze off with just a little bit of personal pride. This was reinforced by the fact that I'd felt it was my lead that had prompted other Dorsets to get into the action, ridding the sky of the remaining flares.

The mess hall stood beside a large quadrangle in the naval barracks and had seating for a thousand or more. The kitchen, or galley as it was referred to, was very modern and staffed most efficiently by the Women's Royal Naval Service. The fact that the Wrens provided for such large numbers did nothing to lower the high standard of their catering, the excellence of which was matched only by the pleasantness of their smiles. I felt that their happy presence in the mess hall each day must have been a kind of welcomed inspiration to the rest of the navy personnel. The way the war was being waged in early January 1941 left little to smile about. Even our vain promises to dress up the Siegfried Line with our washing were now becoming a lot less frequent.

This was the main reason I decided to throw off the blankets and talk Eddie into joining me for something to eat. We were aware that the navy was generally recognised as being the Senior Service, and now, after seeing the way these sailors were fed, while not complaining, we'd come to the conclusion the army could appropriately be considered to be the Cinderella Service.

With just a few hours sleep, I was ready to front up next day for another spell of guard duties around the airfield. The official change-over time was 10 a.m. following a small guard-mounting ceremony. The army post office was now aware of our new location, much to the delight of those keen to get news of their folks in the Midlands. As a rule my mother didn't have a lot of time to write letters, so when my name was called I suspected it must have been something special.

Mum started by saying, 'You'd guessed right. Your Dad's in North Africa now. It was a censored letter, he couldn't say much, but he says he's alright. And you will be pleased to know they've fixed the air raid shelter at last, and Joe, as you can imagine, it makes so much difference being able to stand up in it.

'During a raid a couple of nights ago I lay there thinking about the night we knocked the candle down in the water, then spending the rest of the night with lighting provided intermittently by flashes from the guns of our local ack-ack battery.

'The raids haven't been too bad since Christmas, more of a nuisance than anything else. Larry wrote to us for Christmas. He said his teacher told the class that they all had to write home. He'd rather be home with me he said but it's not too bad. I think it will be better for him when the weather warms up a bit so that he can get out of doors.

I've been told that part of Wales has the most beautiful countryside. If I know Larry, he won't want to come home once the summer arrives.'

After that good news from home, I felt a couple of inches taller as I walked the airfield perimeter, stopping to talk to naval riggers who were working near our gun pit. They'd been patching up shrapnel holes in the fuselage of a Fairy Swordfish aircraft.

These old aircraft looked so outdated, like so much of the equipment British servicemen took into action, testifying to our country's lack of preparedness to wage modern warfare. On the other hand, these same old aviation museum pieces were responsible for crippling the Italian fleet in the Gulf of Taranto less than two months before, and without the daring torpedo attacks launched by similar Swordfish biplanes, Germany's biggest battleship, the *Bismarck*, may well have escaped destruction some four months later.

The men who flew these aircraft were typical of the rest of the navy personnel who were having a short spell away from the sea here at Daedalus. We occasionally shared a table in the mess hall with naval airmen and found them interesting and unassuming in their conversations. They must have been keenly conscious of the likelihood their next meal may have to be eaten in the cramped conditions beneath the flight deck of one of the navy's aircraft carriers. The movement of navy personnel to and from warships was a daily routine at *HMS Daedalus*.

Approaching the pillbox that we were to occupy for the next twenty-four hours, we used duckboards to cross shallow stormwater drains to gain entry. Our sleeping quarters were over a hundred yards away. We pointedly asked the fellows we were taking over from if they'd hit anything during the night and they were quick to reply, 'Philips reckons he did. Mind you, he emptied eight magazines.'

'Is that right?' I asked Philips.

'Yeah, I did,' he said. 'You probably won't believe me. You'll be like this lot, but I reckon I did. Anyway, it's our turn tonight, I'm sure those Jerry pilots won't be too scared to come back.'

We checked out the gun and ammunition and also our field of fire, noting that our previous position was about four hundred yards away, and our current pillbox was situated on the edge of what had been a large field of strawberries. Unfortunately, the local farmer would now have to level out a few bomb craters before any spring crops could be planted. An alert sounded around eight o'clock and it wasn't long before the usual display of lights, along with sound effects, made the pillbox a lot more attractive than our sleeping quarters in the packing case.

There were plenty of bombers around but they didn't seem intent on attacking the airfield. Instead, their attention was directed more towards Gosport, where we'd heard they'd started a blaze at an oil refinery. This, presumably, was responsible for the clouds of coloured smoke that lit up the sky to the east, creating a beacon for the Luftwaffe to home in on.

Since 11.30 p.m., my eyes had been focused on the track that Peter Vandimin would use when taking over from me at midnight. There wasn't a lot happening at that time although the drone of enemy aircraft was fairly constant and still attracting some gun fire.

When Peter hadn't shown up at half-past twelve, I decided to walk to where duckboards had to be negotiated. Visibility was particularly bad, with a light ground mist made worse by smoke. There, close to the drains I found Peter searching in the mud.

'What are you doing down there?' I asked.

'Oh, Lake, I'm so glad you turned up. I tripped on the boards and lost my specs. I've been searching for them for nearly an hour; I can't see a thing without them.'

'I'll soon find them for you,' I told him. 'But first tell me this. What does it mean when there are green and white flashing lights being signalled?'

'Good gracious, are you sure?' He became more than just a little anxious, stepping up his search effort. 'That's the warning of an airborne invasion.'

The glow from the blazing oil refinery and the gun fire aimed at the enemy bombers created a lurid atmosphere around our side of the airfield. On the western side, fires were burning and tracers were being fired at a low angle from several different points.

Peter, seeing that I wasn't overly concerned, soon woke up that I'd been pulling his leg, but he was too upset to raise a smile. After finding his specs he took up his position in the gun pit. He was pleased that it wasn't the guard commander who had come to his aid, or even worse, the orderly officer doing his rounds.

The stand down was signalled around 1.30 a.m. allowing us to get a few hours sleep.

Kenny Baggot approached me after we'd handed over to the new guard and suggested we try out the cinema down the road near the pier that evening. He'd heard a Bing Crosby film was playing and could be worth a visit. I told him that I didn't mind Crosby and that I'd go with him.

Another visit to the naval barracks for our midday meal convinced me that the catering at this establishment was as good as it could get. My only regret was that sometimes I'd walk away from the mess hall and my thoughts would immediately centre on the contrast of my mother's lot back in Birmingham. It was good that she'd said the raids hadn't been as bad in recent weeks, especially now that Dad was in Africa and unlikely to get home for a long time. The tone of her letter suggested she was a little less worried and this could also have been because Larry was now living safely in the Welsh countryside.

Ken and I decided to take a trip into Portsmouth instead of going to the cinema, arriving there early in the afternoon. We'd been advised that if we wanted to avoid being shanghaied into a night of rescue work and fighting fires, we should leave Portsmouth early in the evening and be sure to get the ferry back to Gosport before dark.

One night, the previous week, a group from our company had been turned back from the ferry in Portsmouth and pressed into spending the night fighting fires. There didn't appear to be any shortage of manpower around the docks. Just the opposite. There were sailors everywhere, some of them French, along with a few other nationalities. Plenty of soldiers around too, some engaged in cleaning up bomb damage. Others just sightseeing like us.

We strolled through some of the worst areas of devastation, along roads that appeared to have been recently opened up by bulldozers. There could well have been civilians still buried beneath the rubble we thought, to get to them would have been a mammoth task. Because we only had a couple of bob in our pockets, we walked quite a few miles around Pompey.

At one place, not far from Landport, we realised we must have been close to where the great Charles Dickens first saw daylight. I hadn't read much Dickens, but I knew that most of his tales were penned around poverty and sadness and people generally doing it tough – something that he'd experienced in his own early years.

I remember thinking that if Dickens had been around his birthplace during the last six months he'd have found an abundance of the kind of material he chose to write about. What really caught my imagination was the way in which the local civilian population carried on regardless. It wouldn't have been easy for them over recent months. With raids almost nightly and an occasional alert during the day, it was remarkable that they kept going the way they did. Perhaps, like their football team, Portsmouth had too much pride, not wanting to be overshadowed by other stricken cities such as Coventry, Plymouth and Bristol.

Later, as we strolled along Lake Street, Ken stopped to look in at a tattooist. I'm not sure that it was the window display of tattoos that caught Ken's eye. He may well have been more interested in the attractive young lady who was occupied giving one matelote's arm the needle, as a couple of sailors sat anxiously awaiting her pleasure.

We moved on quickly to make sure we caught the ferry. Failure to have done so could have made us AWOL and I certainly didn't want to lose any more pay.

On a happier note, that snappy little tune "The Ferry Boat Serenade" was all the rage around that time. I can still remember hearing it playing as we crossed the short stretch of water between Portsmouth and Gosport. Despite an undertone of sadness we'd felt after moving around the many areas of devastation, the tune seemed very fitting, almost as if it had been specially written for our day out.

Ken said little on our return to Lee. I got the impression his thoughts were still focused on that tattooist in Lake Street. The bus pulled up near the Tower Cinema and we walked the remaining half-mile along the promenade to our billet, gazing out to sea across barbed wire entanglements and various other obstacles that would confront any invasion attempt. By ten o'clock we were catching up on sleep, something that was beginning to become an important commodity for us at Lee-on-the-Solent.

Next morning, before guard mounting, there was a letter for me containing bad news from home. My mother had only just learned that a mate of mine, Joe Bridgwater, was in hospital with his eyes damaged by an incendiary bomb that exploded as he was attempting to extinguish it.

He'd been in hospital since late November, his injuries occurring during one of Birmingham's worst night raids, and only a couple of nights after neighbouring Coventry had been devastated. This was the raid in which the Birmingham Small Arms factory was hit, killing more than fifty workers on the night shift, some of them teenage girls. The BSA had been among several targets mentioned in recent propaganda broadcasts by the traitor William Joyce, "Lord Haw-Haw", in which he warned us to expect visits from the Luftwaffe.

It took courage to work night shifts in Birmingham's armament factories. Mum's letter went on to say that Joe had just left the Warwick Cinema in Acock's Green Village when incendiary bombs rained down. As a teenager, Joe had enlisted in the Local Defence Volunteers. On this particular night he'd set about extinguishing the incendiary bombs as he'd done on many other occasions during the last few months. Unfortunately for him, that night the incendiaries were different. They were a type that contained explosives designed to seriously injure anyone attempting to deal with them. As the excavators twenty miles away were working day and night preparing mass graves for hundreds of Coventry's victims, Joe had been lying in a Birmingham hospital with shrapnel in his head, arms and chest and had lost his sight. It must have been pretty gloomy for him listening to the Blitz raging outside, not knowing if it was night or day and wondering if he would ever see daylight again.

I remember well the day I received this sad news. It was a typical winter's day. I'd quickly made my way to the gun position so that I could spend a few minutes in meditation away from everyone, knowing this news of Joe would have also caused despair at home. Later that morning we learned that a Royal Marine gunnery instructor would be giving us the low-down on the Lewis guns the following day.

Most of us had already fired many thousands of rounds from these guns. Too bad as it would be on our so-called time off. Lately a lot of our time off was spent cleaning up bomb damage. The fellows didn't object to this when it had been emergency rescue work, or even when we were helping civilians recover personal belongings from their bomb-damaged homes. But there were other times when we were really tired and felt we were just being used as cheap labour.

The Luftwaffe had been fairly active over the last few days and if the weather held we knew we had to be ready for a surprise incursion. It would have really made my day to have got a German aircraft in the sights of my Lewis gun with a chance of bringing it down.

One night, I'd been in the pillbox when Sergeant Spicer, the orderly sergeant paid me a visit. It was about eight o'clock and an alert had sounded about half-an-hour earlier. I'd cocked the gun and not long after, we were listening to enemy aircraft in our vicinity. Moments later I spotted the silhouette of a low-flying aircraft coming almost directly towards our gun pit.

Within seconds, I had the gunsight fixed on the aircraft and asked Sergeant Spicer if I should open fire. Just hang on a bit he told me. Then, as the aircraft came within a hundred yards of being overhead, he slapped me hard across the shoulders as he screamed out for me to open up on it. In seconds, tracers seemed to be ripping through the aircraft's starboard wing.

I'd been about to direct the machine gun fire towards the cockpit when the aircraft released red and green Very lights, quickly bringing our little action to an abrupt end. The aircraft continued seawards. It was one of our own. Despite my anxiety about possible repercussions, there were none, and this incident was never mentioned again.

On odd occasions searchlights had managed to pinpoint a bomber, but seldom led to its destruction. One of those rare occasions was during our twenty-four hours off duty, causing us to be dragged out of bed to spend half the night in search of the crew who'd bailed out. That was the night we found just one enemy parachute on the rifle range at Gosport.

We later heard a rumour that two German airmen were picked up the following morning. Apparently they'd roamed around freely, being mistaken for Allied aircrew. That evening the raiders were back. There was a constant drone of bombers above and around the airbase, yet they didn't seem intent on bombing us. It was as though they were crossing our area either before or after their bombing runs on Gosport and Portsmouth, possibly trying to avoid direct confrontation with flak ships and other warships that were moored to the south and in and around Portsmouth Harbour.

We weren't looking forward to the visit of the Naval armourer that morning. At least six of his guns had seen action during the night. Ours had emptied five or six magazines. At least I'd finally remembered to use my ear plugs. The other times I had fired the Lewis gun, I'd had no access to hearing protection. So the big question - was it too late to use them now?

At this point, I should recount one of the more interesting, out-of-the blue little incidents brought about by the Luftwaffe – things that could only have happened during the Blitz, and for obvious reasons a story I've kept to myself until now. Margaret was one of a small group of very popular women staffing Lee-on-the-Solent's local Women's Voluntary Service canteen. Soldiers were a bit of a rarity in this canteen because it was frequented almost entirely by sailors. After about half-an-hour or so performing lackadaisically on the canteen's small snooker table killing a bit of time away from the mob, Margaret approached me to say she thought the night's air raid was getting worse. If I wanted a cup of tea before leaving, she said I'd better have it now.

As there were only a couple of others in the canteen they'd soon be closing their doors. She brought over my tea herself and I realised she was more than just a little concerned about the raid. She confided how terrified she was during raids. This elegant and very attractive lady must have been at least three times my age, but after listening to her fears I decided I should try to do the right thing and offered to walk her home in the direction of Gosport.

The raid was still going strong as we reached her place, so she asked me to go inside with her and she made me a cup of cocoa. She told me how she hated the thought of being in the house by herself during a raid. It was still continuing an hour later. So she suggested that I stay in the spare bedroom, provided I left the house before daybreak. She told me she didn't want any of her neighbours to see me leaving, knowing that some would be quick to think the worst of her.

During the early hours of the morning, I lay watching the effects of the raids through the bedroom window when a heavy salvo from nearby guns must have come close to lifting tiles from the roof of Margaret's cosy home, causing me to quickly roll over and bury my head into the pillow, fearing window-panes were about to shatter. Within seconds, a fully-clothed Margaret burst into the bedroom, kicked off her slippers and leaped into my bed. She snuggled up beside me and I could feel her body trembling and her pulse thumping away uncontrollably. Mine was too, but I wasn't exactly sure if it was for the same reason. She squeezed the length of her body hard against me and I tried to comfort her. Then, gazing up at the ceiling, I tried to figure out what Margaret's next move would be. I'd been put in a bit of a predicament.

I didn't know whether to attempt to kiss and caress her, something that because of the unusual situation I'd have found very easy to do, despite the generation gap. But I thought this might have further complicated her problems, so I decided to just lay back quietly in anticipation. She then squeezed her chin firmly under mine as her left arm wandered across my chest. She seemed to be intent on trying to position herself under me.

Just as I was beginning to think that this was surely going to become my first real taste of romance, those exciting great expectations came crashing down to earth. She whispered to me to just keep still until her nerves settled down enough for her to return to her own bed. Running through my mind was the thought that those womanising mates of mine back at the billet would never believe it. I'd be the last one in the platoon they'd expect this to happen to.

We lay there motionless, and I had a feeling she wasn't likely to make another move until the air raid eased off. My face was pressed deep into her neatly groomed hair, and I was overcome by a very strong sense of her. She'd suddenly become a lot younger, or, maybe I'd suddenly gained a few years. This was a feeling more intense than anything I'd experienced until then.

About six-fifteen, Margaret came into my room to wake me up. Although a very beautiful woman, she looked tired and drawn this morning. All she said to me was that I'd better dress quickly and get going, and that it would be daylight within an hour. She didn't mention a word of what had happened during the night, and her tone of voice seemed a little more assertive and different now. She politely asked me to go as soon as I could.

The days slipped by. I went out of my way on a couple of occasions hoping to see her again, and, must admit, this had been the motive for a few short sessions on the canteen snooker table. But I was denied the pleasure of her company and we were never to meet again. Other women at the canteen told me that Margaret, at her naval officer husband's suggestion, had left her home and gone to stay with relatives somewhere in rural Hampshire. This news was a disappointment that I hadn't contemplated. Something had given me a strong urge to want to speak to her again.

Was the attraction based on some kind of motherly warmth that I'd seen in her, or was it that army life was advancing my maturity more quickly? My fifteenth birthday had quietly slipped by unnoticed a couple of weeks before.

Now came the morning when we were to get our belated training on the Lewis gun. At 10.30 a.m. about forty men from our company fronted up for the lesson from a senior Royal Marine instructor. It took place on a thirty-yard miniature range situated on the western side of the airfield, one that was used mainly for testing the guns of fighter aircraft.

The instructor was very good and soon got the full attention of the Dorsets. Then unbelievably, almost as if the marine had arranged it himself, a delayed alert sounded simultaneously as a German bomber swooped fairly low across the airfield from east to west, roughly in our direction. The bomber's engines suddenly began to scream out on full throttle just seconds before its nose started lifting skywards and began gaining height.

The instructor hurriedly lifted the Lewis gun off its mounting and raced out into the open area at the side of the range, hoping to get a few rounds off at it. Unfortunately, by the time the raider emerged from a small low cloud it was out of range. The Dorsets were so impressed by the professionalism of the marine instructor that they all stood and applauded, causing him quite a bit of embarrassment, though he couldn't hide the beam of satisfaction that wreathed his face.

Later that day, Ken and I finally made it to the cinema, getting away from the billet before we could be nabbed for other duties. The cinema at Lee was packed with mainly navy personnel, and on account of our late arrival we were forced to occupy seats in one of the front rows. About an hour into the film, a warning flashed on the screen advising there was an air raid alert. This warning wasn't really necessary as we could already feel the vibrations from the raid, which was also causing slight distortions on the screen.

While the acoustics of the cinema would have probably been all right during normal times, the muffled sound of gun fire could be heard almost continually. This was enough for a few of the patrons to take casual glances around the theatre, no doubt curious to see what effect the raid was having on the others. The interruption was enough to make anyone feel a bit edgy. However, we were determined to enjoy the film. As far as the army personnel were concerned, when you're paid two bob a day it isn't easy to walk out of a show before you got your money's worth - for Goering or anyone else.

With about ten minutes of the film left to run, there was another warning. This time we understood the raid was close. I can still remember looking round at Ken, who appeared to be quite rapt in the show. We decided to see it out, as did a couple of hundred others.

When the film ended, we wasted little time getting to our feet, but as we'd been sitting in one of the front rows we found ourselves near the tail of a very slow-moving queue that was making its way along an aisle towards an exit at the rear of the theatre. There were indications that the raid was hotting up.

And then, catastrophe! There was a tremendous explosion and the whole building shuddered violently, bringing down pieces of plaster and broken light fittings. I tried to dive between seats, expecting the roof to cave in as a powerful slightly delayed blast ripped through the foyer, smashing through glass swinging doors and hurling people into heaps in the aisles and among seats.

There were screams coming from beneath a cloud of dust that had enveloped the cinema entrance, some of it drifting down over the rear seats of the theatre. Many people were in a state of shock, among them was a woman about forty, who struggled to her feet screaming abuse at sailors whom she alleged, had broken her arm in their haste to get out onto the street. Others had been hit by debris and looked stunned, unable to comprehend just exactly what had happened, while a few just stood there and tried to wipe dust from their eyes, too disorientated to move.

Ken and I had been literally picked up by the blast along with several others and thrown forty or fifty feet down near the foot of the screen. Fortunately none of us sustained anything more than a few small cuts and bruises. Ken was very lucky — there was a nasty little gash above his left ear that could have easily been much worse.

The explosion, we were to find out, had been caused when a stick of bombs had straddled the promenade, one of them exploding not far from the front of the cinema.

We eventually got out on to the street. There were dozens of people lying near the cinema entrance waiting for first aid. As we hadn't had much sleep the night before, we wasted no time making our way along the seafront back to our billet. We found out how lucky we'd been by staying to see the end of the film. We saw tons of debris covering the promenade. Some had actually landed close to the back lawn of our billet.

One bomb had exploded on the edge of a swimming pool only a couple of yards from the ocean side of the promenade. Had we left the movie following the second warning, we'd most likely have been somewhere near this very spot.

Before mounting guard next morning, I spoke with Eddie Atkinson and a mate of his, Dickie Bird. They reckoned they'd found the ideal hide-away and only a few hundred yards from our billet. They, too, had been feeling the effects of the lack of sleep brought on by having to do endless additional duties on their time off.

This spot sounded like the ideal place to catch up on lost sleep so we decided we'd check it out. The few raiders that did make an appearance that night were at long intervals, but just frequently enough to spoil any chance of getting our heads down. We'd decided against firing our gun, even though some of the bombers appeared to be close enough to hit.

The marine instructor had told us that unless we could actually see the target, or were convinced the aircraft was well within range, we'd most likely be wasting ammunition. This was slightly different from our initial instructions advising us that the magazines for our guns contained twice the recommended number of tracers. Their presence in the sky would act as a deterrent, making it harder for enemy pilots to select targets around the airfield, especially during low-level attacks.

And so, after another sleepless night, we crawled back to the billets. I was hoping Ken could join me when I went to look over the promised haven that Eddie had found. But this wasn't to be as Ken would be making his way back to Portsmouth for a special reason. He had plans to get in the queue to have that lovely young woman etch something on his arm that would remind him of her beauty for the rest of his life.

News had just reached us that one of the next few days would be spent on the rifle range at Gosport. We also heard that sometime during the following week, the Royal Marines band would take part in our marching drill. This caused a ripple of excitement because this particular band was one of the best in Britain. I hoped the Dorsetshires wouldn't cramp their style.

After dining at Daedalus, Eddie and I ventured along the promenade, crossing the slipway that provided access for seaplanes in and out of the naval base. It was on the western side of the slipway near the water's edge that Eddie and his mates had found a track that led to a very secluded section of the beach.

Two hundred yards further on we arrived at what must have been a popular swimming spot before the war, with a row of bathing huts positioned just above the high-water mark. Apart from the huts there was nothing except an old clinker built dinghy about ten feet long, as well as a couple of oars.

This place certainly looked as good as Eddie had led us to expect. The huts weren't locked and contained beds, and all in all seemed too good to be true. Barbed wire entanglements made it inaccessible to civilians but there was a possibility sailors may have been using the beach huts for a hideaway. The state of the track near the slipway suggested it had been used more regularly.

For about a dozen of us, this little retreat soon became a real haven.

Chapter Six: Tragedy Awaits

From my tour of inspection with Eddie, it seemed this out-of-the-way spot would be an ideal place to catch up on lost sleep. There was a chance to write a few lines home in private and, if we were still at Lee-on-the-Solent when summer arrived, we might even be getting our clobber off.

Later that evening, Kenny Baggot got back from Portsmouth with a work of art on his left arm just below the elbow. It was in the form of a brightly coloured dagger with a scroll intricately woven around it, with the words, Death Before Dishonour, leaving no question as to the depth of Ken's integrity. And all for seven shillings and sixpence. Ken and I talked for an hour as we lay on our beds awaiting the all-clear.

An alert had sounded around 7.30 p.m. but there hadn't been much action over Lee, the glow in the sky to the west suggesting Southampton was being targeted. Before getting to sleep around eleven o'clock, I found myself very concerned about my hearing. The conversation with Ken had worried me.

There was clearly a decline in my ability to hear certain words, and I suspected I was suffering from the effects of weeks of firing the Lewis gun. The logical thing would have been for me to see the medical officer, but I was scared he might ask too many questions. While the MOs at the recruiting depot had given the impression they were on a commission for every recruit they passed fit, our battalion MO might see things in a different light.

The following morning, a terrible rumour spreading through the billets made me momentarily forget my hearing problem. We'd heard that a heavy anti-aircraft shell had come down in a house occupied by the Wrens, exploding in their dining room and causing many casualties. Although most bad news was hearsay, later

I learned that this tragedy had actually happened. On November 23, 1940, ten women of the WRNS were killed.

The bleak and overcast day seemed to reflect this sad event. Windy and rainy weather cut short the guard-mounting ceremony. Only the thought that the Luftwaffe would likely be grounded by poor flying conditions gave some solace to this most inhospitable day.

During early afternoon, despite the bad weather conditions, five or six naval aircraft arrived out of the haze, wasting no time taxiing over towards the main workshops on the southern end of the strip. They appeared to be Blackburn Skua or Roc dive bombers. Perhaps there was a carrier off the coast.

We'd find out in the morning when our sailor friend came to service the gun. He seemed to know everything that went on at the naval air station. The Wrens had sent out the most delicious evening meal for the guard. What a pity they didn't come along and dish it out as well; that sure would take the gloom out of the day. I suspected the Wrens treated us army blokes better than their own navy colleagues. Of course, this may have only been my imagination, but I was sure these young ladies couldn't possibly have treated anyone better than the way they spoiled the Dorsets.

Rain was still falling as we changed the guard, raising hopes that our trip to the Gosport rifle range might be called off. When Ken asked CSM Trusler if the target practice was still on, he found himself the subject of a five-minute lecture, during which the sergeant major explained that the Germans kept fighting regardless of weather conditions.

'So, it's up to us to be able to beat them even if the pitch is a little rain-affected,' the CSM told Ken. 'You do understand that, don't you Baggot?'

Ken didn't need the lecture. If our visit to the range had been cancelled, it would have meant waiting five or six weeks before it was again made available to our company. But Ken, like the rest of us, was dog-tired. When would we get our time off?

Our day at Gosport left little doubt about the accuracy of our American rifles. What a pity they were so awkward and lacked the smart lines of the British Lee-Enfield. Conditions on the range that day had been very poor for good shooting. Intermittent rain, a light variable crosswind along with poor visibility that came into play at all distances over a hundred yards, left some Dorsets wondering if perhaps they should have enlisted in the Artillery. Others appeared to have had real sniper potential. Philips for example, scored very well having a natural passion for any kind of weapon, an interest that hadn't extended into any other areas of his infantry training.

On our way back to Lee-on-the-Solent, we had to call in at the Gosport airfield where other men of the Dorset regiment were engaged in a role similar to our own. We were able to speak to Cyril Barton, another Brummie, who had a brother called Donald in our company.

Two nights before, they'd been badly shaken and were lucky to have survived a stick of bombs that had exploded less than forty yards away, in a line parallel to their row of Nissen huts. The bombs left huge craters and scattered tons of debris around and on top of their quarters.

Before leaving we managed to catch up with ex-RSM Geard, who was now a platoon sergeant at Gosport. He seemed very happy and was in a jovial mood, showing not the slightest resentment of his demotion.

Bleak weather that marred our day on the range came to our aid that night by keeping the Luftwaffe away. It was our first real full night's sleep in our new home by the sea.

There'd been good news that day. We heard that British and Australian troops had captured Tobruk. It's about time we had a win I thought, and wondered if the old man's unit had been one of those involved.

And, from home there was more good news, if you could really call it that. My mate Joe Bridgwater was out of hospital at last, with partial vision in one eye. My mother told me that Joe had been given an ultimatum by an eye specialist. Unless Joe allowed him to remove the more badly damaged eye, he stood the real possibility of becoming totally and permanently blind. This must have been a terrible decision for a young, good looking teenager like Joe, to make. But he really had no choice. Although he still had shrapnel in his head and chest, his sight had improved a little in the short time since the operation, which must have been heartening for him. Knowing Joe's determination, and with a little bit of luck, his footballing days might not yet be over.

What a difference a day makes, certainly on our airfield. It was such magnificent weather I felt like a tourist as I made my way around the perimeter towards my nocturnal home away from home.

The change in the weather not only improved my morale but by late afternoon there was little doubt that flying conditions would remain good for that night. "Cockney" Worthington would be sharing the chores with me and had already agreed that I should do all the firing, if we had to use the gun. The weather was still very cold, and Worthington was aware it took just two magazines to warm the gun barrel sufficiently to raise the temperature of the gun pit for an hour or so.

So, I was hoping that by ten o'clock the following morning my knowledge of London would be broadened, and not just about the underworld where Worthington maintained he had served his apprenticeship.

Although the stage was set for a visit from the Germans, by 8.30 p.m. nothing had happened, so I got my head down after supper, knowing that I was on the midnight till 2 a.m. stint.

Worthington's voice was the next thing I heard calling out, 'Come on, Joe, they're here, come on!'

It then dawned on me that I was on guard duties. In seconds I'd grabbed my helmet and rifle and found myself standing with Cockney alongside the gun before my eyes were properly open. Half-an-hour later, searchlights momentarily had what we thought must have been a wayward barrage balloon in their beams. It was very high and a fair distance away. A few seconds later searchlights were once again able to pick it up, this time long enough to identify it as a landmine swinging lazily beneath a huge parachute drifting northward towards Fareham. It was still very high, but we were relieved when there appeared to be an easing in the gun fire as it passed immediately above us. Several minutes later to the north there was a huge flash on the horizon followed by the rumble of a blockbuster detonating a few miles away. We'd heard about landmines that the Luftwaffe used frequently on London, Birmingham and other cities, but this had been our first sighting.

During a lull in the action, we sat along the wall of our gun pit and were once again entertained by a nightingale. Its lilting song echoed out across the nearby meadow from a hedgerow just outside the airfield perimeter. It sounded quite close to our pillbox. This beautiful bird seemed to be carrying out a protest. It was telling us we had no right to be creating thunder as there'd been no clouds to warn of pending storms; it was wrong to create spasms of daylight through the night, the nocturnal hours belonging to their domain and we had no right to interfere.

This lone nightingale continued on and on, as though it really did have a complaint to lodge, carrying out its unanswered plea right up until we fired on the enemy bombers returning from the north. Then once again that charming little contact we'd had with sanity was swiftly brushed aside and gun fire contemptuously returned to take control of the night.

The next morning we'd planned to move to our beach resort before we could be nabbed for other duties. It was a pleasant day so a few of us took an early lunch before heading off along the beach track.

It was still only early February and much too cold to take our shirts off, but such a far cry from the towpath of the Grand Union Canal, where many of us had learned to swim on odd occasions, going through the ritual of fending off dead animals or oil slicks before entering the murky water.

We slept most of the afternoon, with the added luxury of each of us having our own cabin. Not long after the light started to fade, our little patrol gathered up rifles and gear then headed back towards the billet feeling happy with our few hours rest and recreation. And so as the days slipped by, the pattern of our leisure time included a couple of afternoons at the beach each week.

Our spell with the band of the Royal Marines went off very well. The scruffy Brummagem lads rose to the occasion, I thought, and I heard that our commanding officer had been quietly pleased with our turnout. As for the Royal Marines, they were truly a great band. It certainly gave me pleasure listening to the high standard of their memorable performance.

It came as a surprise a few days later to learn that, just when our battalion seemed to be showing a new awareness of esprit-de-corps, we were asked whether any of us over the age of twenty would like to transfer to another unit. For those who accepted the offer, every effort would be made to relocate them to a unit of their choice.

The opportunity was immediately taken up by a small number and it was expected that during the following months departures would become more than just a trickle. In the meantime, our task of defending the naval air station went on. Although we realised the threat of invasion was now slowly diminishing, we were told the Dorsetshires' presence on the airfield was still an integral part of the area's security.

A surprise visitor to my pillbox next day was Company Sergeant Major Trusler accompanied by the orderly sergeant. The CSM jumped into the gun pit showing a keen interest in the gun and its field of fire. He then went below to check out ammunition and iron rations.

Back in the gun pit, he put to me a number of questions in quick succession. 'When did you last fire the gun? How many times have you been sure of hitting a raider?'

I made sure I didn't mention the night when I was pretty certain I'd hit one of our own aircraft.

'Do you always use ear plugs?'

Then quickly, without changing his tone of voice, the CSM asked, 'What year were you born?' He didn't bother to wait for my reply as he'd climbed back out of the gun pit. I wondered what had prompted him to pop a question like that. Perhaps he thought I'd be among those applying for a transfer in the coming months and couldn't believe I would soon be twenty.

Something told me I would be accepting that offer of a transfer to another regiment when my "official" army age reached twenty in a couple of months' time. In the meantime I began making enquiries to find out in which battalion of the South Staffords my mate George Bowman was serving. I tried to convince myself that with a bit of luck I might even get in to the same company as George.

Air raids around Lee-on-the-Solent were being seen more as a nuisance now, compared with raids of the past. The ferocity of earlier attacks had eased in recent weeks. While alerts were still interrupting a good night's sleep for many people, enemy aircraft numbers had decreased, as had the damage they caused. Last night had been no exception when the guard stood-to for three hours or more listening to aircraft criss-crossing Lee, almost as though the Luftwaffe was using our airspace for training purposes.

Next morning, after the guard hand-over, five of us decided to visit our secret beach retreat. The weather looked good, although a little chilly. I couldn't wait to get my head down for a few hours. Despite the presence of naval personnel, some of them officers, no one questioned our right of way as we casually strolled across the slipway and on to the beach track. In less than half-an-hour we were all sleeping soundly.

After a good three hours, the high-pitched whine of a motor torpedo boat cruising just off shore woke us from our slumber. Worthington was already up and snooping around like he was participating in some sort of treasure hunt. He was a man of endless energy, but not very industrious in its application.

Easy-going Jack Shuttleworth was skimming stones over the smooth water of the Solent, just as he'd done from the towpath of the Grand Union Canal a couple of years earlier. He was all smiles and obviously enjoying the relaxation.

As for me, I was content to sit on the steps of a dressing shed and gaze out across the water, filling my lungs with beautiful sea air and still finding it hard to believe I was actually living at the seaside. The events of the last couple of months had reassured me about my soldiering, bearing in mind that I was now a fifteen-year-old.

Dickie Bird called out that they needed my help with the boat. The old dinghy was small but quite heavy. However, we were eventually able to snig it across the shingle beach into the sea. I remember hopping in first and sitting up in the sharp end, closely followed by Jack and the Cockney, leaving Dickie and Eddie to steady the boat, before attempting to climb aboard themselves.

By the time Dickie was seated, it was obvious there wasn't going to be enough freeboard to take Eddie as well. Eddie thought differently, since it had been his idea to put the boat in the water. He tried desperately to pull himself up onto the stern, before being pushed off by the boots of Jack and Dickie. The dinghy was by this time in about three feet of water, so when Eddie finally parted company he was waist deep in the briny. It was not the ideal situation for a cold Tuesday in February, even though it was the south coast of England. It wasn't surprising to then hear Eddie, standing wet and shivering, shout abuse at the rest of us, his language echoing his feelings.

Soon after the laughter died down, we took the dinghy a couple of hundred yards out from the beach, leaving Eddie to dry his clothes. Jack was urging us to row over to the Isle of Wight, but we'd only gone about half-a-mile when an increasing ripple looked like testing what little freeboard we had, so we decided to head back to shore.

Then, almost as we turned, we heard what sounded like gun fire. We all immediately turned our attention towards the sky, but couldn't see anything suggesting a raid. I did notice a small cloud of whitish smoke or mist which seemed to hang close to the ground in the direction of the promenade. We were too far away to pinpoint the spot, but it must have been a couple of hundred yards or so east of the slipway.

Just before we got back to the beach, the skipper of an approaching naval patrol boat had his machine guns pointing very war-like towards our dinghy. Then, closing with us and checking our identity, he said he thought it very unwise for us to be playing around in that locality. Before heading off at high speed, he advised us to head back to the beach the same way we came. Twenty minutes later we put the dinghy back above the high water mark, collected our rifles and gear and began making our way back towards the slipway.

We'd been feeling pretty pleased with ourselves, having had a decent sleep and some time to unwind. But after the naval officer's advice we thought it unlikely we'd be putting the boat in the water again. As our little safari moved across the slipway near the water's edge, we saw a very serious-looking Sergeant Major Trusler heading in our direction, his eyes unmistakably focused on me.

The first words he spoke when about fifteen yards from us were, 'Oh, so now we know, Joseph Lake.'

'And what is it you know, Sir?' I asked the CSM.

'That you're still with us, so it must have been Atkinson that blew himself to pieces a little more than an hour ago.'

The sergeant major's hands were cupped across his body just above the waist. They held the shattered remains of an army boot that contained what appeared to be part of a person's foot. There was also what looked like the messy remains of part of a scalp with an appendage that resembled an eyebrow. By using that eyebrow CSM Trusler had been able to narrow down the number of men from our company who fitted the description of the unfortunate victim. He knew then that it had been Eddie who'd become our company's first fatality. His next of kin could now be notified, before finding out when and where his funeral would take place.

The CSM was obviously very upset and told us that he would like to talk to each of us later. I'd never seen the sergeant major looking like that before. It was as though he'd just lost his own son.

Jack Shuttleworth was the first to speak as we walked back to the billet.

'It was fate that took Eddie,' he said. 'Just because we kicked him off the boat like we did, there's no reason for any of us to feel responsible for his death or that we'd even contributed to it for that matter.'

Dickie Bird wasn't very talkative. He'd probably been closer to Eddie than the rest of us. But, because it was Dickie that put his boot up to prevent Eddie getting on to the dinghy, it's possible his action would remind him of the tragedy for years to come.

Worthington was looking more reserved, saying that it wasn't necessary to talk like that. 'The war got Eddie, and it's going to get a lot more of us before it's over. We'll all miss him. He was a good mate, but that's the way it is in wartime.'

'What do you reckon, Joe?' said the Cockney. 'What do you think?'

'I agree with you,' I told him, 'but I'd like to know how it happened. Eddie wasn't a fool. How could he lose his life in this way? Is there something about the defences along this foreshore that we've not been made aware of?'

Guard mounting on Wednesday was a welcome relief and an opportunity to get away from the billet. I understood why Company Quartermaster, Staff Sergeant Coombes, wasted little time removing Eddie's belongings from our room.

But it was the callous way he'd gone about it, when he suspected we weren't being co-operative, that caused the stir. He'd reminded us that, as far as the army was concerned, we were all just another bloody number. Then before leaving he'd asked if there was anything else belonging to Atkinson. When he received no reply he gazed suspiciously around our room for a few moments before heading back to company headquarters.

When I looked out across the airfield from my pillbox my thoughts were with Eddie, and I wondered how his passing would affect the rest of his family. He'd only ever mentioned his father and I had a feeling his early years hadn't been all on easy street. One of the reasons I'd felt sad over Eddie was that things were starting to look a bit brighter on the home front. Like many others in the battalion, Eddie, who was an eighteen-year-old, had enlisted at a time when a German invasion looked imminent. But we'd recently heard a rumour that the Germans had now decided against their planned invasion.

Eddie had gone, not knowing that Britain had most likely weathered the storm, thanks to the fighter pilots of the RAF, and to a lesser degree, the often-overlooked solidarity of the women in the worst of our blitzed cities, particularly London.

These women, civilians like my mother, played an important role in keeping the home fires burning. This they'd done commendably, and many of them while their husbands were away on active service. They may not have shared in the glory of winning the Battle of Britain, but indirectly these women had played a major role in its outcome.

Looking back over the previous six months, it seemed we'd overcome the setbacks of June, 1940, when England looked as though it would be the next country to be overrun by the Wehrmacht. U-boats were still taking a heavy toll of shipping, causing severe shortages of just about everything.

Churchill's memorable speech glorifying the "Few" had been made just a couple of months before, and, by-and-large, air raids didn't seem to be as bad. People were learning to live with setbacks. Bad news had been on the top of the front pages since the war started, so unless it was bad news of a very personal nature it often passed with little more than a sigh.

The good news was that Birmingham hadn't had a bad air raid for nearly a month now, as my mother told me in her last letter. This would have given the Brummies a chance to clean up the city a bit as well as time to dispose of unexploded bombs. The future looked anything but bright and you could hardly say there were any signs of light at the end of the tunnel, but morale appeared to be just as high in the February of 1941 as it had been the day the war started.

Chapter Seven: For Eddie, a Last Parade

Most of Britain's adversities during 1939-40 came about because we'd entered this war totally unprepared. Now, even though more than seven months had elapsed since the army's humiliating evacuation from Dunkirk, the dire circumstances that had existed throughout Britain meant that implementing counter-measures were still slow. For security reasons and morale, civilian casualty numbers were hushed up during the Blitz, but it was generally understood that well over forty thousand civilians had died in raids on England during the autumn and early winter of 1940.

There were now many senior units of the British Army that, in the coming months would be quitting their amateur status, so to speak. Revised training programs would help put them on better war footings, their battle training now being modelled on what had been learned from the Germans when they'd overrun France.

The transition to wartime soldiering had not come easily for some of the regular units of the British Army. Many of them had grown used to the imperial "peace-keeping" function, which they'd fulfilled creditably during the inter war years. What little action they'd seen, if any, had usually involved the quelling of insurrections and riots, striving to keep apart various sectarian factions while endeavouring to maintain and keep open good lines of communication.

In places such as India, the North-West Frontier, the Middle East and Northern Ireland, the role of the military had been more that of a policeman's rather than that of a soldier's in wartime. Too much training had been spent on the parade ground. While this may have been good for disciplinary purposes and no doubt produced ceremonial displays that warmed the heart of many a high-ranking officer in a peacetime army, much more needed to be done in this new era of the Blitzkrieg.

On Churchill's orders things were beginning to change. From now on there would be less spit and polish and more sweat and blood. The demand now was clearly for gladiators, not administrators. I began to realise that later in 1941 I would most likely be joining one of the units that had made the transition.

Around eleven o'clock on the morning following Eddie Atkinson's death, I was checking out the Lewis gun, the weather suggesting we'd most probably be using it that night. Of course, around the gun pits the main topic of discussion was Eddie.

So far there had been no official statement about his death, and for that reason his mates and others were convinced we were shortly to witness a big cover-up. Peter Vandermin and Kenny Baggot were sharing guard with me that day. The last time I'd shared guard duties with Ken, I'd come close to bringing down one of our own aircraft and Sergeant Spicer who'd urged me to shoot at it that night, may well have come close to being reduced to the ranks.

Not long after dark, enemy aircraft started crossing the coast at high altitude, but because there was no gun fire Peter, Ken and I remained seated on the side of the gun pit. It seemed like a re-enactment of most recent raids, incursions designed to create disruption more than damage and inevitably reducing the opportunities for us to use the gun.

Because the raid seemed to be directed more towards the Portsmouth area, it was possible to get some sleep after eleven o'clock, and when we'd found out what our program was to be for the coming day it was just as well we had.

Details were released about the commanding officer's wish that Eddie be given a full military funeral to take place at the Gosport cemetery, with Eddie's father in attendance. There was also a request from CSM Trusler that Eddie's mates take part in the ceremony, either as pallbearers or members of the firing-party. And, since no one except some of the regular soldiers in the unit had ever participated in such a ceremony, rehearsals would begin right away.

Nothing could have compensated Eddie's father for the tragic loss of his son. He showed little emotion as he stood beside the grave, looking every bit a Brummie in his dark overcoat and grey cap with traditional white silk scarf. Although he stood there a very lonely man, it was only when the Last Post sounded that he appeared a little overcome; his short frame wavered slightly before he quickly braced his shoulders, his eyes gazing fixedly ahead.

I thought it ironic that Eddie's last resting place should have been directly between those of two German airmen. There were, in fact, many members of the Luftwaffe and other servicemen among recent interments in the plot containing Eddie's grave. Despite the short notice for the ceremonial parade, I imagined the commanding officer would have been reasonably satisfied with the result. It was as though Eddie's popularity had been acknowledged with a special effort by the rest of the fellows in the unit. I know that was exactly the way I saw it.

***

Those memories of 1940 during the time of the Blitz are still so clear. Those early war years had been exciting times that often brought much laughter, sometimes tears, and for a few, a sadness that would take a while to dispel. I began writing to enlighten my grandson Jack about how different our lives had been. But from here on is another story.

On June 22, 1941, the Germans launched "Barbarossa", their attack on Russia, giving Britain and the Commonwealth a welcome ally. Although our situation was still only slightly better than hopeless since a large proportion of the Luftwaffe had been moved to Eastern Europe, raids on British cities started to ease somewhat.

Nine days later, and while still at the tender age of fifteen and a half, I moved to Whittington Barracks at Lichfield, the traditional home of the South Staffordshire Regiment, where I later caught up with my good mate, George Bowman.

This time we were guests of the RAF at Thornaby airfield, a Lockheed Hudson station near Stockton-on-Tees. George and I were in the same company for about five months before he was transferred to the Black Watch. He was soon to be sent to North Africa to join the 51st Highland Division.

The United States, after sitting pat for more than two years, and capitalising on the trading of mainly obsolete armaments to Britain and the Commonwealth, was forced into war on December 7, 1941, following the surprise bombing of Pearl Harbour by the Japanese. The war that started in Europe with the ruthless bombing of Warsaw by the Germans in September, 1939, had now become worldwide.

By March 1942, the German Army was beginning to get bogged down in Russia and later would face a humiliating defeat at Stalingrad. Combined with other set-backs around the Mediterranean, the threat of a German invasion of England now seemed well beyond the capabilities of the Wehrmacht.

My sixteenth birthday had passed three months before and I was now getting progressively bored with continually passive roles such as beach patrols and general guard duties. One such job was to spend every other night on a small air strip where we stood by in readiness to ignite drums of tar and other inflammable materials, part of a ploy to mislead German bombers. We were to set the drums alight if the Germans appeared intent on attacking the vital Dorman-Long steel foundries that were not far from our Nissen hut accommodation, near Grangetown.

During our regular marches through the surrounding mining districts, which included the villages of Brotton and Skelton, we brought much laughter to the villagers who opened their doors to spur us on, especially when we were echoing our plans to "Hang out the Washing on the Siegfried Line".

Though the Americans had now been drawn into the war, the possibility of us ever getting close enough to the Siegfried Line to carry out those threats still seemed way beyond our imaginations.

In North Africa, General Montgomery was beginning to make his presence felt but it was still too early to suggest the tide may be starting to turn in our favour. Eventually, with the thought of moving forward into a more enterprising role I applied for a transfer. I then volunteered to join the recently formed airborne division, and moved to Carter Barracks at Bulford on Salisbury Plain with the 2nd Battalion of the South Staffordshires two months later. This was a glider battalion and one of the four battalions that made up the 1st Air Landing Brigade, commanded in 1942 by Brigadier "Hoppy" Hopkinson.

After only a few months in the brigade, I was convinced it must have been one of the finest of the units that were in the middle stages of a new and much revamped British Army.

When I'd applied to join the airborne forces along with a mate "Thommo" Thompson, we were interviewed by Major Fox at the Zetland Hotel which overlooked the seafront in the small north-east Yorkshire town of Saltburn-by-the-Sea.

After the interview it was arranged that Thommo would join the 2nd Battalion immediately, but because I, along with Private Don Dorman, was halfway through completing a Physical Training Instructor's course, we would be on a second draft about six weeks later. Don, a future Birmingham City and England footballer, and I were instructed to meet up again at Newcastle on Tyne's YMCA canteen before heading off to Bulford, where I'd hoped to tag along with Thommo again, a few weeks later.

On our arrival at Bulford, Don and I were assigned to the same platoon in C Company. I immediately set about finding where my mate, Thommo, could be found. When I asked an old friend, Bob Edwards, he advised me to contact Private Bensley in D Company.

'Why Bensley?' I asked.

Bob then told me the sad story that it was Bensley who'd just returned from a week's special leave granted for volunteering to escort Thommo's coffin to his family just a couple of weeks before. It came as a bit of a shock for me to learn that Thommo had only recently died in a glider accident.

During our interview, Major Fox had explained to us that gliding was now regarded as being out of its infancy in the British Army. But, I was to learn in the coming months, there were still many experimental exercises being carried out.

Finding out about Thommo's death took the edge off my hidden excitement at joining the airborne forces, quite apart from the fact I'd been counting on him to show me the ropes in my new battalion.

Soon after my introduction to flying, I found that with most new gliding techniques used in wartime, such as tight formation flying or variations in dive-approach landings and so forth, pilots fully tested gliders laden with sand bags and several other forms of ballast.

But, before the gliders could be certified and actually put into general use, they had to be tested with glider pilots flying "live" loads, and that's where our presence was required.

We were paid an extra shilling a day above standard army pay for serving in a glider unit in the spring and early summer of 1942. Company Sergeant Major and regular soldier Joey Glynn of C Company would often say that we should be paying the army for all the excitement we were getting.

Later, I was to learn the accident that claimed Thommo's life had occurred during close-formation flying, a part of gliding that I wasn't particularly keen on. This was an exercise that got a bit dicey especially during poor weather conditions and if there was going to be any excitement, it would most likely occur after gliders parted company with their towing aircraft.

This I found out for myself in the months ahead. I learned also that, because the army wished to expedite training programs for glider pilots, they'd persuaded the RAF to allow flying to continue at times when conditions were difficult.

I can remember a couple of occasions when I'd boarded a glider and RAF officers openly exchanged words with our officers, declaring that flying should be called off for the day. Such confrontations helped add a little more interest to what we were already expecting to be an exhilarating outing. This inter-service antagonism was usually played out in good humour, although the RAF really did hate to have their high standards called into question by the army.

This was the case at the Kidlington airfield where I'd had my first gliding experience, on a day that had been a memorably bad one for me. On that particularly cold and wet morning, after losing half my week's pay playing pontoon while waiting for a light fog to lift, our small Hotspur glider carrying eight of us finally got off the ground.

A few seconds after becoming airborne I remember making a fool of myself when I'd asked some of the other blokes if they knew anything about the big manor house I could see through the mist a couple of hundred feet below.

'Don't show your bloody ignorance,' was the retort. 'Surely you recognise Blenheim Palace?'

I paid more attention to Winston Churchill's birthplace on future flights.

After only a few weeks at Bulford, I found no trouble settling in to the high standards of the 2nd Battalion. Although I was a sixteen-year-old, I felt able to hold my own with the rest of the fellows, especially in shooting, cross-country running, forced marches and in fact all other tests of endurance.

The airborne forces endurance tests in one form or another were often a weekly occurrence, some of them requiring the utmost effort. The battalion was also particularly strong in boxing and was matched against an American airborne unit that had only recently arrived in the UK. Of the ten bouts on the program that evening, we lost only one, but, in all fairness to the Americans, they'd sportingly agreed to enter a team at very short notice, without any preparations.

After witnessing the professionalism of the battalion boxing team, which was coached by senior PTI Ryan,

I made sure the promoters were well aware of my capabilities in the ring. The only boxing I'd competed in was at a schoolboys' club and I'd been wise enough to leave it at that. Quite apart from being among a terrific bunch of blokes, I had taken an instant liking to the excitement of gliding, and flying generally.

Some of my happier days in the army were spent around the airfields of Kidlington and Brize Norton. Also, many of the South Staffords in C Company came from the Birmingham area and in my platoon there were quite a few who hailed from nearby Walsall.

Our company commander was Major M. W. Brennan, who was later to act with great courage in the first hours of the Sicily invasion in July, 1943. His glider was one of many that came down in the sea close to the coast, forcing him to swim ashore under fire. Then, while at first armed with only a pistol, he was able to personally account for more than twenty enemy prisoners.

I can still remember clearly one particular Saturday morning at Bulford when I'd requested forty-eight hours compassionate leave. I'd been asked to try to get home to assist Henry, one of my mate's brothers, who wanted me to give evidence on his behalf in a legal problem he'd got himself into back in Birmingham.

As there'd been no one at the company office who could sign a pass for me, Staff Sergeant Probert suggested I find C Company's 2IC Captain Robert Cain, as he was the orderly officer that day. After I tracked him down to the ablutions block, he agreed to sign a pass but told me he wasn't going to get out of the bath.

'You get the pass book and bring it here,' he said.

Less than two years later, as Major Robert Cain, he was awarded the Victoria Cross at Arnhem. He was also given the great honour of being the one selected from the many millions of men and women of the British and Commonwealth's Armed Forces to lead the Victory Parade in London following the end of the war.

Since I've mentioned Major Cain, I should also mention Sergeant John Baskeyfield, who was in the same platoon as me during 1942-3, and who also won a Victoria Cross at Arnhem in 1944. While at Bulford, John and I were good mates although we never knocked around together. In fact, there'd been a little rivalry between us over our abilities as marksmen, always good-humoured of course.

Best part of a year after joining the airborne forces we learned that the red beret was to become the standard headdress for our division, and while the red beret was well accepted generally, months later it was to cause repercussions for me. My problems surfaced late in 1942, after a few days at home that followed a week's intensive gliding at Kidlington.

It was during that short spell at home that my mother must have realised I was no longer in a unit that had been formed in an emergency to help thwart the German invasion threat of 1940. I didn't know at the time, but the red beret, and the glider proficiency badge that I'd proudly worn on my lower left sleeve, had prompted Mum to get a letter off to my father in North Africa.

Apparently, my father had suggested to Mum that she should let my commanding officer know that she was concerned for my wellbeing and that she should question what kind of unit I was now serving in.

It was only many years later, that I learned that Major Brennan had answered Mum's letter, telling her that the CO had no intention of forcing me to leave the battalion. And as I'd shaped up satisfactorily to all their requirements, he advised my mother that Lieutenant Colonel "Grubber" Jones, our battalion CO, was of the opinion that I should stay in the 2nd Battalion. He'd also told my mother that, because the battalion would be carried into battle by air, there should be no cause for alarm. The general officer in command would ensure that the lives of his men would not be thrown away on any futile mission.

His letter must have put my mother at ease.

During April, 1943, I arrived home, telling my young brother Larry that I was on embarkation leave and expected to be leaving England soon, possibly for the Middle East.

'That's what you think,' he told me, and went on to reveal what had gone on behind my back. I was truly lost for words and considered returning immediately to my unit. I felt I'd been betrayed.

The 2nd Battalion of the South Staffordshires was a regular army battalion that had returned to England in 1940 after completing most of a routine tour of duty in India. The battalion had been brought home prematurely in order to go directly into France to join the BEF. As with most county regiments, the battalion took pride in its strict observance of British military traditions, some of which took place on Christmas Day when all commissioned officers reverted to mess orderlies, waiting on, and helping serve dinner to all other ranks. It was also traditional that the commanding officer personally served Christmas dinner to the youngest soldier in the battalion.

On a happy Christmas Day, 1942, I can remember sitting down for dinner at Carter Barracks with about a thousand others, enjoying the usual antics and carryings on as we watched these regimental customs being carried out enthusiastically by all the commissioned officers of the battalion.

Suddenly, a dinner plate that was almost hidden by a huge leg of turkey was placed in front of me, the size of it prompting several arms to reach out from around the table in a bid to take possession of it.

'No, don't take that one,' hinted the slightly tipsy voice of Major Brennan, who was now standing directly behind me. 'That one's Lake's.'

He'd obviously filled the plate himself. If I'd had a better understanding of regimental traditions that day and been less taken in by the size of the leg of turkey, I'd have realised then, that my real age was no longer a secret at battalion HQ.

Some years later, I learned it had been arranged after Mum's letter to Major Brennan, that I should leave the 2nd Battalion until I was old enough to meet the airborne forces minimum age requirement.

My platoon commander, Lieutenant Longman, assured me that Major Brennan had agreed that I could

2nd Btn,
The South Staffordshire Rgt.
c/o A.P.O. Nottingham
8th August '42

Dear Mrs Lake,

Many thanks indeed for your letter telling me all about your son who is now in this Battalion.

It is a slight surprise to be told his correct age, although of course it is quite obvious that he is only a youngster. That fact will however remain a secret for the moment as it would be unwise to declare that he had made a wrong statement on enlistment. Quite apart from that the Commanding Officer and myself have no intention of letting him go as he is turning out to be a very good soldier and I feel if there were only more of his type in the Army and other Services today whose only thought is to do his best without thought for himself then we should not be long in winning the war.

With regard to going abroad it is of course not possible for me to say much as to our future but I can assure you that your son will not be sent off in a draft from here and that on the whole I should not worry too much. One day we will all go abroad and then we'll know that the war will soon be over, but your son will be older then.

With regard to his being in the Airborne Forces, that also should also be no cause for anxiety. We have in command one of the finest Generals in the Army today and it is quite certain that he will not commit his forces to undue danger when the time comes. The fact that we are carried into battle by air and not by sea is really nothing to be unduly worried about.

Thank you once again for your letter and please rest assured that your son will be looked after and that you have every reason to be proud of him, although no doubt, a little anxious.

Yours sincerely,

M.W. Brennan, Major

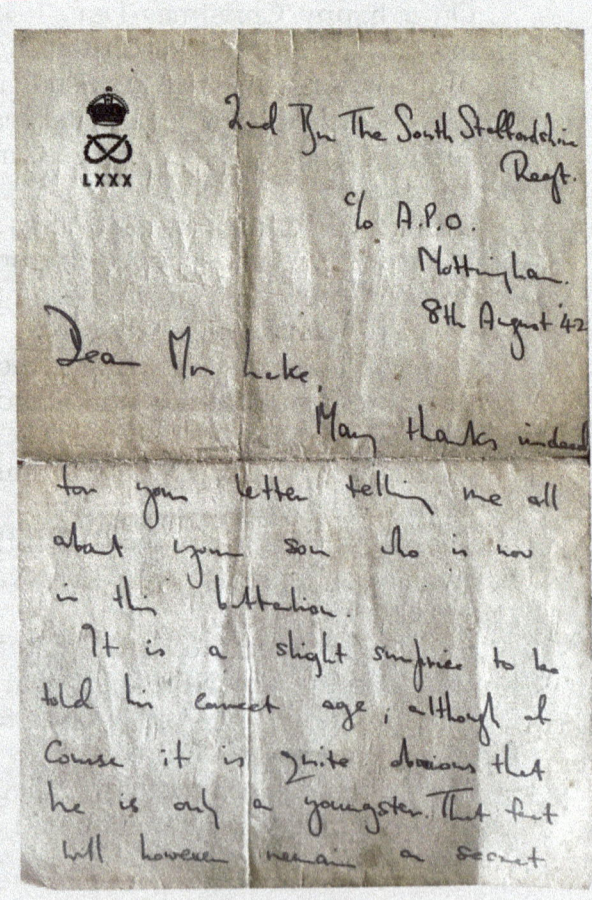

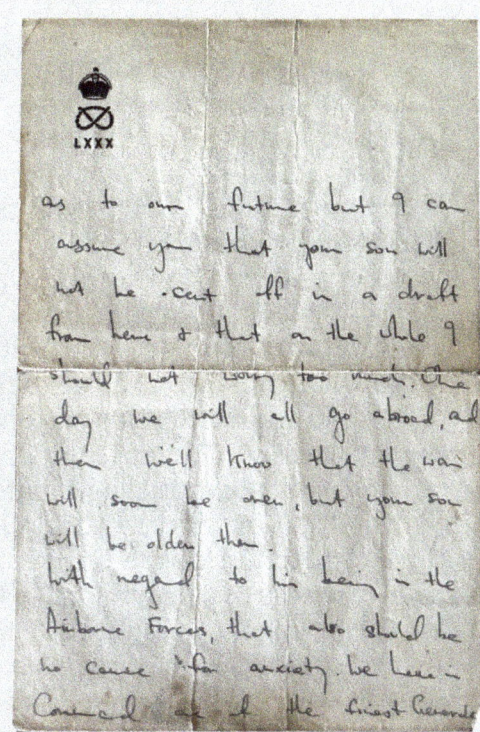

Official recognition of Joe's under-age enlistment in the form of a letter to Joe's mother, Leah Lake, from Major Brennan from the South Staffordshire's Second Battalion.

At that time in August 1942, Joe was only sixteen years old and had become a Red Beret in the Glider Battalion after almost two years as an infantryman. Brennan promised Joe's mother the Army would take great care of her young son.

rejoin my mates in C Company, in the March of 1945, on reaching nineteen and a quarter years, the airborne forces' minimum age.

Not long after that devastating news from my brother Larry in April, 1943, I was sent back to temporary regimental headquarters at Norton Barracks near Worcester, where my new job was assisting in the training of recruits.

Then early in 1944, along with half a dozen other men of the Staffordshires, we were moved to the south coast, where we waited to reinforce one of the assault battalions which was about to cross the Channel. By then I'd turned eighteen, finally, and legitimately old enough to be an enlisted soldier. Soon, I would be taking a farewell peek in the direction of the quickly fading English coastline from the bow of a heavily laden US infantry landing-craft.

By June, 1944, I would be on my way to Normandy and wondering if I would ever see my family again. Would I ever enjoy another cold, wet Saturday afternoon with mates on the wind-swept bleachers of Villa Park? Was I ever likely to be putting football togs on again? These questions, along with many other misgivings, I never had to seriously consider before.

Chapter Eight: From Teen Soldier to Sniper

But I almost didn't make that Channel crossing in June, 1944, as part of the Normandy invasion.

A week or so earlier, I was in Birmingham, quite unexpectedly. My father had sent a telegram to say he'd arrived home from the Mediterranean war zone, and would very much like to see me if it were possible. But he'd heard most army leave had been cancelled. My commanding officer, though genuinely sympathetic, was unable to authorise a short leave pass as we were in sealed camps a couple of miles off the south coast. He was well aware our next move was going to be across the channel.

We knew we were soon to be heading off on a mission that, as infantrymen, and, in all probability, would be a one-way trip for many. So, I decided to take a huge risk. I might never see Dad again, so I decided to give him an opportunity to see me in uniform, since it could well be the one and only chance he'd ever get.

Being aware of the situation regarding security along the whole of the south coast of England, I knew it would present a real challenge for me to get home and then get back into camp without blotting my copybook. Regarding army intelligence, I was aware that occupational currency in the form of French francs had been deposited in a temporary vault that had only recently been dug inside our guard-tent. But I also knew there was never the slightest possibility of me mentioning this to anyone. Apart from that, I really knew nothing more than the entire population of southern England.

My infantry training was called upon that Friday night, helping me negotiate a couple of high barbed-wire fences in darkness without being challenged by guards. Close to midnight, after a quick, uneventful round-about trip by way of Winchester, I was relaxing on a platform at Reading Railway Station awaiting an early morning connection that would take me to Brum.

So far, so good, I thought. But I'd been kidding myself.

Just minutes later, I was apprehended by a very diligent police sergeant who thought I might have been up to something, stealing from mail bags perhaps. After I showed him the telegram and told him my father was also a sergeant and wore the same First World War ribbons as he, the tension eased somewhat, and he became more co-operative. He advised me not to walk down the platform near the station entrance as military police were standing at the lower level near the main gate and he didn't think the Redcaps would show me the same amount of sympathy. I didn't tell him I was already aware of their presence, and that was why I'd been standing in total darkness at the far end of the long platform.

After questioning me on a couple of other issues before looking at my return ticket, he left for a few minutes and I began to wonder if perhaps he was actually setting me up for the Redcaps. But it wasn't so. On his return, he advised me to continue to wait out of sight until my Birmingham connection arrived at 1.30 a.m. He would then flash his torch if it was all right for me to get aboard.

Before he left, he gave me some friendly advice, warning me that under no circumstances should I leave the train at Birmingham's Snow Hill station. If I did, he reckoned I'd be picked up by military police immediately. It had been a long day and I was very tired and must have fallen asleep as the train pulled out of Reading station, but luckily I awoke at daybreak when moving through Birmingham's outer suburbs near Stechford, a couple of miles or so from the centre of the city.

The train was moving faster than I would have liked, but, after the police sergeant's warning about Birmingham's Snow Hill station being a definite no-go area, I was left with little option. So, while still feeling a little drowsy, I drew upon experience I'd picked up at Hardwick Hall's airborne forces training school more than a year before, and leapt from the train.

It was actually travelling much faster than I thought,

and I rolled seventy or eighty feet down a fairly steep embankment. I managed to get back on my feet just a little ruffled up and shaken. Thirty minutes later, I was on an Outer-Circle bus heading towards Acock's Green. The rough-and-tumble down the railway embankment must have added to my now rather fugitive-like appearance. On the plus side, I hadn't started shaving by then and since I was the only one in uniform on a bus filled mainly with war workers, I sensed that I'd suddenly become the focus of their attention.

A conductress, about thirty, or maybe a bit younger, moved casually along the bus to take my fare. She looked me in the eyes as though she was well aware I shouldn't have been away from my unit. Then, speaking in a friendly tone of voice that sounded like she could have easily been my older sister, quietly asked me how far I was going. On hearing my reply she turned away, moving further down the bus without taking my fare. It seemed as I was in khaki, this part of my journey would be as a guest of the Birmingham City Council.

And so, after an absence of four years, I was finally able to sit down with my father and enjoy breakfast with the rest of my family. My brother John, who was now a pilot in the RAF, had been able to get leave for the weekend. It was great to see Dad and Mum. We knew that Dad had had a couple of bouts of malaria while in North Africa, but that had been more than a year before. He looked very well that day.

Dad was surprised to see me because he knew all leave had been cancelled. He was a bit of a stickler regarding discipline, so he was quite concerned about me getting home without a pass and about the possibility of me being charged for being absent without leave from my unit.

On Sunday afternoon, John and I, feeling contented and pleasantly relaxed after spending a few hours with Mum and the old man, made our way to Snow Hill Station to get back to our respective units. While walking along Colmore Row towards the station, we were approached by a couple of Redcaps patrolling near the churchyard. Understandably they weren't very happy with me not having a leave pass, but they eventually allowed me to go my way unaccompanied after my brother John, who was senior in rank, agreed to take full responsibility for me returning directly to my unit.

The trip back to camp was uneventful, except I had to walk cross-country for the final half-mile. This I chose to do after seeing military police vehicles on roads nearby. Getting back into camp that night proved more difficult than getting out, and gave cause for me to draw further on my experience with the Red Berets.

It was well after midnight on Sunday and I'd decided to re-enter a heavily barbed-wired section of the camp that I knew was occupied by part of the Canadian 9th Infantry Brigade. These particular Canadians were men of the North Nova Scotia Highlanders, and, as I'd expected after a little chat, were more than helpful in getting me across to my own part of the camp.

At daybreak, my tent mates were quick to let me know my absence had not been discovered, but told me also that it was just as well I'd got back. My name had been among those listed for fatigue duties at seven o'clock that Monday morning. During the afternoon, I was feeling a bit tired but pleased that I'd been able to see Dad.

It also felt good that my mates had to admit that I'd been successful in the trip they'd all thought would have been a venture destined for failure. However, at around 4 p.m., I received a message to say my presence was required at the camp office immediately. The corporal wasn't able to tell me what I was wanted for, but he did say he understood it was reasonably urgent.

Fifteen minutes later, I was standing in front of the camp commander's table as he read out a report that had come from military police by way of the senior officer for security in our region. There wasn't anything I could say. He'd been well aware of my desire to get home to see my father. Everything was clear-cut.

On Tuesday morning, I was charged but was lucky, I suppose, to get off lightly with just ten days field punishment. The light sentence presumably was to make sure I'd be available at short notice to move onto landing craft with the rest of my unit.

Had I been in the German Army, the seriousness of the circumstances that existed at that time may well have got me shot. I'd heard the CC had been requested from higher up the line to explain the breakdown in security and had been asked what sort of action he proposed to prevent a repetition.

I felt a little sorry for the camp commander, who was a well-liked officer. If I had known my trip to see Dad would end this way, I certainly wouldn't have made the journey. My misdemeanour had caused the CC much embarrassment.

That afternoon, I sat a little remorseful on an old iron bed in a huge solitary cell in one of the old Napoleonic forts at Gosport. It was either Fort Rowner or Fort Brockhurst, I can't remember which. But there is one thing that I can still remember clearly; the bombs that struck the fort, probably the second night of my short stay. Luckily for me they detonated about fifty or sixty yards from my cell. The following shock waves travelled through the ramparts of the old fort, rattling the heavy iron door of my dungeon-like accommodation.

I'm pretty sure that old iron bed lifted at least a foot off the flag-stoned floor when they hit. The fort was a very solid structure and some of the walls were ten or fifteen feet thick and covered by mounds of earth. The remainder of my ten-day sentence was spent in long hours cleaning up debris around the officers' quarters, where most of the damage had occurred and I heard there had been casualties among the officers.

Generally speaking, I was given a pretty easy time by the guards. They thought I'd been a bit unlucky, after learning of the circumstances that had led to my becoming their guest. I returned to my unit feeling fit and well and sorry for the trouble that I'd caused, but also pleased that none of my family was likely to find out about my being charged.

Soon after returning to my unit, I left the small port of Newhaven on an American LCI heading for Sword Beach on the Normandy coast, and once there quickly forgot about the trip home.

During my final weeks in England, I'd been transferred temporarily to the North Staffordshire Regiment along with about twenty other young infantrymen and in particular, Private George Churchman, who was soon to become a good friend. Few, if any, could have been more than eighteen-year olds, and to me they looked remarkably raw, even their khaki and webbing equipment still had that QM store look about it.

Our early days in Normandy were taken up in various roles, escorting prisoners, getting first-hand experience lifting German mines, and generally assisting beach groups. Then, after just a couple of days spent closer to our forward positions while getting used to continuous shelling and mortaring, we were sent as reinforcements to a village a mile or so southeast of the recently captured township of Hermanville, and there, joined 8th Brigade, part of the British 3rd Infantry Division on July 12. George and I attached to the 1st Battalion of the South Lancashires.

At the time of our joining 8th Brigade, they'd been smarting from the loss of so many of their numbers during savage fighting near Lebisey and surrounding villages and woodlands just to the north of Caen, which was the town that had actually been 3rd Division's D-Day objective.

We'd joined the brigade just prior to its preparation to move off on what was to be one of the biggest offensives of the Normandy campaign, an attempt to break a stalemate and extend the bridgehead several miles to the southeast. Three armoured divisions were to spearhead the attack along with several infantry divisions into an area east of the River Orne, our objective expected to be almost completely neutralised by a thousand heavy bombers of the RAF.

Shockwaves made the ground vibrate where we stood. We watched the heart-warming sight of the beginning of a massive air assault as we waited from a high spot a couple of miles to the north, for the order to move off into the fray. Our morale that had been cautiously high, was raised a little higher by the inspiring remarks of a couple of our senior officers. They were of the opinion that nothing could survive bombing of that scale, telling us our task should be comparatively easy. They were to be proven wrong. "Operation Goodwood" held many surprises.

The day was hot and within half an hour the additional weight of basic ammunition pouches, containing Bren gun magazines, slung loosely around my shoulders had me perspiring excessively. I was beginning to show signs of exhaustion. Perhaps I wasn't as fit as I thought.

After reaching the start line, sporadic enemy shelling began to make the situation more serious as officers looked across towards other units on our flanks, awaiting the signal to begin the advance. We then moved off at a steady but brisk pace over a mile-and-a-half or more, in rough extended order, across open undulating wheat and grazing country. We weaved our way cautiously while regularly having to go to ground for cover.

The immediate terrain which included a couple of shallow, sunken lanes was gradually sloping down towards our objective. We were soon passing some of our own tanks that had been brought to a halt, a couple of them smothered in flames and belching sickening black smoke. This sight, together with constant incoming shells, many of which were air-bursts detonating forty or fifty feet above the ground, suggested to me it wasn't going to be the walkover senior officers had told us to expect.

Near a very exposed farm track about a hundred yards or so away to my left and slightly ahead, I caught a glimpse of a tank crewman who seemed to be effortlessly engaged in performing a grisly tarantella in a bid to extinguish flames that had enveloped his head and shoulders. I felt a sigh for him and thought someone nearby should have gone to his aid.

But for this attack over ground, which was void of any kind of cover, we'd all been ordered not to stop to assist anyone, not even casualties within our own platoons, until we'd cleared the open ground that extended right up to the edge of our objective. And while German anti-tank gunners appeared to be having a field day, about three or four hundred yards ahead, through a smoky haze that was beginning to lift, several groups of unarmed German troops came into view. They'd begun emerging from the lightly wooded area that we understood was going to be close to the limit of our initial attack. They appeared to be in shambles, a couple with their hands above their heads, some of them assisting the shocked and walking wounded.

Within minutes we were moving through them as though they weren't there, leaving them to make their own way into captivity as they cowered beneath an increasing number of airbursts being put up by their own guns. These Germans were moving very hastily under the circumstances, obviously realising each stride they were taking in the direction of our guns was enhancing their prospects of surviving the war.

Close to our battalion's first objective of the morning, and in my haste to gain cover from fairly intense enemy shelling, I realised I was struggling to keep abreast of the rest of my section. I endeavoured to move at their pace and had to force myself to subconsciously emulate most of their immediate actions. I half vaulted and half rolled blindly over a very long, low brick wall that ran along the edge of an orchard and found myself almost at grips with a German soldier. Lying face down and appearing well above average size, he was rigged in the smock and helmet of a paratrooper. My instant reaction was that I had to kill this paratrooper before he could kill me.

At this crucial moment, in the half exhausted state I was in, my arms seemed to fail me. I was suddenly paralysed as I struggled to bring my bayonet into play. My head and shoulders had fallen heavily across the lower part of his body, his oversized type of well worn jackboots seemingly fixed loosely under my armpits as I drew on the last bit of energy I had left to get clear of him.

But I needn't have worried. His body seemed limp, and he was lifeless. It looked as though his life had been snuffed out by blast as he'd sought cover from the massive air bombardment. His judgment had probably cost him his life by selecting the wrong side of the wall, a little more than an hour before our large-scale attack had even begun.

In the meantime, shelling and mortaring eased enough for me to lift my head and take a quick glance around. The surrounding area was one of complete devastation. I lay there for a few minutes after making sure the combatants in field grey who were much too close for comfort, weren't going to suddenly raise their heads and get back in to the action.

After a few moments listening to threatening rifle and machine gun fire close by, and feeling more than just a little uneasy, I decided to take leave of the corpse. My exhaustion was compounded after trying unsuccessfully to retrieve the Schmeisser from underneath the dead paratrooper. I didn't want to lift myself too high above ground into what seemed like random small arms fire. Then moving carefully for about twenty yards, and hugging the ground strewn with debris from small trees and dead livestock, I eventually reached the edge of a large bomb crater.

I positioned myself among huge clods of warm, moist earth that were still emitting slight traces of vapour. The churned-up earth around the crater provided me with cover from view. It was an excellent place to observe the movements of the rest of my sparsely deployed platoon, a platoon where all except George Churchman were complete strangers to me. I most certainly didn't want to be accidentally left behind in this particular spot where nothing had survived the hellish destruction from the RAF's saturation bombing.

Heavy enemy machine gun fire continued to rip through the tops of small apple trees just a few feet above the ground, but the odd single shots that rang out were more likely to bring a frown and prompt an inquisitive peep to where a few of the others in the platoon were taking refuge. Continual mortaring and sniping made it necessary for us to wait until dark before we could leave our cover to start digging trenches in some sort of order, placed roughly in accordance with the platoon sergeant's strategy. His motives gave the impression he'd been told to have us ready to repel an expected enemy counter attack. For the rest of the day we made use of bomb and shell craters for cover. It must have been well after midnight before we'd finally got a better hole and were organised sufficiently enough to carry out a roll-call and do a rough ammunition count. It seemed the Germans had moved quickly following the bombing and were able to reoccupy parts of the devastated area, including two or three high spots that controlled all the ground our battalion had gained during the onslaught.

Days following the attack, the situation was particularly grim, thunderstorms helping to make matters worse, especially where shelling and intense sniping prevented us from burying the dead. There was increasing stench from rotting corpses, together with that of cordite and the drying sap from trees that had been ripped apart by constant shelling. It certainly didn't help complement a diet of mainly bully beef and biscuits.

To make things worse, we had to brew the unpopular and equally unpalatable compo-tea on a Tommy-cooker at the bottom of a muddy slit trench. The situation deteriorated even further, after rain turned the shell and bomb craters into breeding ponds for millions of mosquitoes. Most of us had never experienced mosquitoes in plague proportions. Within hours any exposed skin became the target of the little bloodsuckers and there was nothing we could do about them. We soon realised the mozzies were sharing their affections with enemy dead as well as various other bloated carcasses that were widely strewn, just yards from our trenches. Very soon everyone had infections on their necks and wrists from the bites. Those showing the worst effects, including two blokes in my company were evacuated out of the line for medical attention.

'Lucky buggers,' we all thought. 'Why couldn't I have been one of them?'

From our trenches, we looked out over the field-grey uniforms of the enemy. They'd become more noticeable having been washed by recent thunderstorms. The bodies had been laying there a couple of days bleaching in the sun, and exposed to the hot Normandy weather. Most were Panzer Grenadiers, probably from the 21st Panzer Division who'd been confronting our division since the second day after the Normandy landing.

The Panzer Grenadiers, and many of their heavy tanks, had been caught napping by hundreds of four-engined RAF bombers as the Germans leaguered close to the edge of woodland. The result was disastrous for them. Many of their Mk4+Mk5 Panzers had been thrown around like matchbox toys a little over an hour before we launched our attack to occupy the area. My slit trench for the following three days was just a few yards from a forty-ton tank with its rear end partly inside a huge bomb crater.

The blood-saturated torso of a crewman hung ghoulishly from its turret, the head and arms having been ripped off by the blast. Several other crippled tanks and dismembered bodies lay in close proximity. During my four years of soldiering I'd never witnessed or even imagined carnage like this.

There were several unsuccessful day and night attempts to collect the dead for burial. We were frustrated by intense sniper activity and mortaring. We were told an armoured bulldozer would be brought in to push the bulk of the enemy corpses, and dozens of dead farm animals into the nearest bomb craters. The crater would then be covered to help reduce the risk of disease.

The trenches we occupied were in a bomb and shell devastated apple orchard that stretched across dozens of acres. We'd been warned by our superiors, that if you presented a target to the enemy during daylight in our partly-exposed position, our wounds were considered to be self-inflicted.

So, we were very cautious to only venture from our trenches after dark. The nearby enemy machine guns were firing on discretely selected fixed lines, and they blasted away continuously at our position during the day and cunningly at irregular intervals throughout the night.

I apathetically dug a spoon into a less-than-warm tin of Irish stew that had just been hurled across to me from a neighbouring trench. Throwing tins of food from trench to trench was the only way we could safely get anything to eat during the hours of daylight.

There I was, snatching a quick meal after partly regaining my lost appetite, stooping down in the bottom of a shallow storm-saturated slit trench, my grubby and very muddied trench-mate keeping dog-watch a couple of feet away.

He was so tired he could hardly keep his eyes open, but he was going through the motions of scanning enemy positions. Fate caught up with him later that week after his long-standing request for a transfer to the "carrier platoon" was finally accepted.

I'd only known him for two days, but long enough to learn how resentful he'd become about living in a hole in the ground. He'd been edgy and was still suffering from the effects of the close fighting. He'd been particularly affected when the heavy enemy tanks overran one of B Company's forward platoons.

Before the Germans were forced into retreat, the Panzers had repeatedly swerved their tracks across their long narrow trenches on the edge of the woodland near Lebisey, crushing and burying alive a couple of his mates.

He would have been happy to be out of the trenches when a few days later he left our platoon. He joined the crew of a Bren gun carrier that was running the gauntlet to bring rations and ammo up to our forward positions during stand-to time, just after dark. The sound of its engine brought on a mortar stonk within minutes of its arrival and the carrier took a near direct hit. He was killed instantly.

The carrier caught fire and within seconds the exploding fuel, along with its cargo that included PIAT anti-tank ammunition and phosphorus grenades, put on a brilliant multi-coloured firework display. We listened to a variety of munitions exploding as we hugged the bottom of our trenches. Although it never went up in one big bang, it did in fact go on for a good part of the night. The enemy took full advantage of this to hammer our illuminated positions.

Over the previous few days, our battalion had been subjected to what seemed and sounded like a never-ending symphony in heavy weaponry, with variations loosely orchestrated and wilfully performed subconsciously by gunners on both sides of the line. An occasional added crescendo was included on our behalf from warships lying just off the beaches.

As we were so close to the enemy positions, had one of those naval missiles fallen a little short of its target the affects on us would have been catastrophic. We were forever awaiting a prelude to the haunting discord that filled the air following the sporadic firing from the nearby Nebelwerfer batteries.

After a short delay, their rockets, regularly brought a shower of debris, or worse into our trenches.

All this was accompanied by an overpowering stench from rotting farm animals and countless German corpses. I crouched awkwardly, trying to squeeze myself a few inches deeper into the ground, and realised I was unintentionally vying for space with another young fellow who was our platoon's most recent arrival from England.

After a day in the trench in a heavily mortared area, he'd been more than willing to partake his first rum ration under the stars, as were were peppered by big and small fragments of hot Krupps steel. The enemy's seemed intent ongradually reducing what little normality, remained to us. We were dug in around verdant and typically Norman farmland.

I'd been silently visualising a traumatic Wagnerian scene against a woodland setting just a couple of miles away to the south east. An endless stream of rockets continued from the deadly and mobile multi-barrel Nebelwerfers. They were being fired with a fair degree of accuracy in our direction.

My tired and over-strained imagination found it hard to believe that these perpetrators of hell on earth were also akin to the maestro who gave music lovers the *Moonlight Sonata* and the symphonies of Mendelssohn and Schumann. I had to acknowledge that without the kin of these cold-blooded militaristic Germans, I'd have been denied many pleasurable hours spent in meditation with Bach.

I now realised I was a different person from the one who'd pestered that sergeant recruiter back in Birmingham nearly four years before.

I also noticed that morale had taken a turn for the worse. Those tired and weary footsloggers were beginning to sense that our hanging out the washing on the Siegfried Line was going to take longer than we'd thought.

After several days of endless bombing and shelling and many casualties, any further forward gains by our Division appeared to be remote. Most of us had been under the impression that we might finally break out of the bridgehead and see a reduction in enemy shelling. But our big push had suddenly ground to a halt.

General Montgomery's British Liberation Army, the BLA, was facing the cream of all enemy forces in Normandy. With several superbly equipped SS Panzer divisions at their disposal, we now knew the Germans weren't likely to give up any more territory to the British without another major struggle.

There'd been a thunderstorm and heavy downpour. Private George Churchman and I cleaned our rifles, while stooped down near the entrance to a small trench which we had only recently taken possession of. The trench was cut into the bank of a partly-sunken, shallow lane.

About a dozen enemy fighter aircraft came in low towards us, and strafed our positions. They were the first I'd seen in formation since joining 8th Brigade. The aircraft were met by a heavy response from Corps and Divisional light ack-ack batteries, as they crossed above a small timbered ridge, entering the perimeter of the bridgehead. The sudden, intense gun fire prompted the Luftwaffe pilots to immediately break their tight formation before independently bombing and raking our trenches with machine gun fire.

I came close to death that day. In our haste to take cover, we hurled ourselves into the small dugout. George, who'd been replacing the bolt in his rifle, inadvertently squeezed the trigger before realising his rifle was loaded. The bullet left holes in my tunic and a slight skin graze on my left side, just above my waist. For a few seconds, I was speechless.

'Hey! Whose bloody side are you on?' I screamed out, in a knee-jerk reaction, before realising that he'd had an even bigger shock than me.

His tired and weary eyes looked me over in horror. He was so relieved he hadn't killed me. We didn't have much to talk about for a while. I remember feeling a bit sorry for him, knowing the circumstances could so easily have been reversed. However, it took several hours and a couple of enemy mortar stonks before our friendship returned to normal.

I was now an eighteen-year-old, and, like most Brummagem lads who were brought up during the Depression years, I had acquired a good appetite that could be easily satisfied. The Irish stew, as was the treacle pudding and a few other lines that came up regularly with our compo-rations, wasn't too bad, but nowhere near as good as Mum used to make. Like all army rations, the taste and quality seldom varied. Over recent days this little part of Normandy was certainly not the place for anyone who was the slightest bit finicky.

It had been a month or so since I'd experienced the luxury of a proper wash as the never-ending hostile conditions prevented us from taking off our boots. Thankfully, the toothache that had helped to take my mind off other things over the last couple of days had gone. I'd finally managed to yank out the troublesome tooth during a mortaring late the previous night.

Earlier that evening our platoon sergeant made a hasty visit when he brought along the welcome rum ration to my trench just after dark. He appeared a bit uptight and even had a go at me for not having my mug ready. Like the rest of us, he tried to keep time spent on top of the ground to a minimum, in this the most hellish of places, so Sergeant Rooney's feelings were quite understandable.

I considered mentioning my tooth problem to him before having second thoughts; the rest of the platoon weren't going to get a laugh at my expense. It was generally understood that nothing short of a substantial flesh wound would justify a visit to our regimental aid post, something that would add to the burden of our overworked medics.

When talking of time spent on top of the ground, most of us felt that our company runner might well have earned an award each day we'd occupied this particular area, as belligerent an area as any in Normandy at that time. His dedication hadn't gone unnoticed though. This unassuming fellow's deeds were eventually recognised but not until months later when we were near the Belgium-Dutch border. The company runner and the driver of our small water-tanker who both spent a lot of time in the open, were each awarded a military medal. Decorations were given on a quota system and their heroism quickly accounted for our batallion's allocation. It took a long time for the medals to arrive because of the bitter fighting that took place on D-Day and the days following the landings. It was still possible to get an occasional glimpse of the long brick wall I'd hastily scaled for cover during the big attack a week or so earlier. It was a little over two hundred yards away to the north, between mounds of earth heaped up around bomb craters.

The wall was about four feet high and its ornamental wrought iron railings had been removed, no doubt by the Germans to be converted into munitions. The wall ran alongside a gravelled road that led away from a village and up to a two-storey house that appeared to have miraculously escaped the bombing with only minor damage. Some companies of our battalion were now well entrenched seven or eight hundred yards beyond the wall. The corpse of the paratrooper I'd grappled with was still awaiting burial, along with many of his comrades.

This little bit of Normandy, which was partly timbered and on the edge of open dairy and grazing country, would have been quite picturesque before large swathes were mercilessly converted into a moonscape by the RAF. The nearby area included a now deserted and very ghost-like village of stone cottages and farms surrounded by cider apple orchards and low stone walls. It was not unlike the villages you'd see in rural Devon or Cornwall.

Around one side of the village were some large trees, a couple of which had survived the bombing and had soon become the centre of our attention as we scanned the landscape for snipers. Two or three days into our occupation, our battalion commanding officer was one of the many to die there. The colonel was shot through the neck, adding to the ever-increasing number of men, particularly officers, falling victims to snipers.

For about two weeks my company was hustled and shuffled around, occupying various unsavoury locations within the area of devastation. Then there was a sudden enemy action and the Germans were accurate with their shelling. We were continually bombed and shelled, but thankfully during the action, we were still able to hand over our trenches to the men of the 49th Division.

This sudden attack confirmed our beliefs that the Germans could observe nearly all our battalion's movements before and during the changeover. Although I'd been in a few nasty places since first setting foot in Normandy, this past fortnight seemed a hell of a lot longer. I've often wondered if the French civilians returning home to their properties after the war would ever know of how many soldiers found a final resting place within their fields.

The second day after leaving this very keenly contested battlefield east of the River Orne, 3rd Division moved to the sheltered west side of the bridgehead where it was comparatively easier going for us. The bridgehead was close up against the American sector. From there, we began trudging the dusty roads towards the town of Vire, and later on to Flers.

We, in 8th Brigade, were still putting in attacks every other day, but on a much smaller scale. Sometimes it was only of company strength. Panzers weren't such a threat. The only ones we'd seen since our arrival on the west side of the bridgehead, had been those abandoned, perhaps after running out of fuel. Others showed evidence of being crippled from the air by the rockets from RAF Typhoons.

Casualties were much lighter now. Although our platoon was only a little more than half its full complement of thirty-three, reinforcements didn't seem to be arriving. Because it was easier going to some extent, it also meant that I could at last get to know the names of a couple of other chaps in the platoon.

Soon after arriving on the western side of the bridgehead, our brigade had moved quickly, walking through rain and thunderstorms while moving cross-country for two days and nights in long extended patrol-like formations. We made contact with the enemy again in the afternoon of the second day, their accurate mortaring quickly putting an end to the short break our stretcher-bearers had been enjoying. This urgency we were told was to help make sure the town of Vire would quickly fall to the Allies, our division eventually sharing in its liberation.

That night, my section made the most of a long, deep German-dug trench that had been evacuated by the enemy only hours before. It was on a hillside to the south-east and not far from Vire. We knew that our battalion would be leaving its positions before daybreak for a dawn attack.

I thought I was being smart when I stood my shovel in ground close to my trench, before hanging my webbing equipment on it to make sure I'd be untroubled to move off quickly in darkness next morning. During an enemy bombardment that night, a shell detonated close up to my trench, a splinter from it ripping the handle off my shovel. It also left a gaping shrapnel hole through the centre of my small pack and its contents. Enemy gunners obviously didn't require co-ordinates for these particular trenches.

We were in position at daybreak and moved off under the covering fire of the Vickers machine guns of the 2nd Battalion, Middlesex Regiment, a style we'd now become too familiar with. At first, we were accompanied by Sherman tanks manned by the County of London Yeomanry. But, after just five or six hundred yards, two of the four tanks on the eastern side of a narrow country road had disappeared into sunken lanes, in what appeared to be a small pocket of bocage-type terrain.

By the time our attack had covered a little more than a mile, there was only the distant sound of the remainder of our tank support amid increasing and well-directed enemy shelling. We were then pinned down for nearly an hour by accurate shelling and mortaring. I tried to gain cover by lying in a shallow depression along the edge of a small cabbage-patch at the rear of a cottage, as I watched my mates tirelessly digging in, along a nearby hedgerow.

We anxiously waited for someone to scream out orders for us to get moving again. As the German gunfire intensified and my mates dug in further, I was reminded of what an important piece of equipment a shovel was to an infantryman – and not just for burying the dead.

What had started an hour or so before as a casual stroll through beautiful countryside turned into a desperate struggle to dig in and find cover. We were spurred on by the all too familiar cries for stretcher-bearers. When mortar bombs and shells began detonating in tree-tops very close to me, I knew it would be another of those long days as I lay there without a shovel.

Our platoon eventually took our objective without the aid of our so-called tank support. There'd been light casualties throughout the attack and we'd had to leave behind a couple of men with shrapnel wounds. We moved quickly past the other wounded who'd been left by the leading platoons. Some of them were already on stretchers and others lay motionless beneath blankets. For some, these dreaded blankets would inevitably become a symbol of the final request made on their behalf by B Company's hard-line quartermaster. Thanks to one of these unfortunate men, I was in possession of a shovel again.

The casualties were scattered at various intervals along numerous thick hedgerows awaiting field ambulances. Our advance was taking us progressively further and further away from accessibility to transport so it could take a critically long wait for the wounded to be picked up. We maintained our momentum, overcoming a few rearguard delaying attempts by a disorganised German infantry. They seemed of a much lesser calibre than their comrades we'd faced earlier during our recent actions east of the River Orne.

Hardly anyone in our platoon now discussed life before the landings, or even what had happened to them yesterday or the days before. Most talk and thoughts focused on the present and what was likely to happen within the next few hours or on what tomorrow and the day after, might bring. There was the odd person in the platoon who'd acted more inscrutably, no doubt secretly questioning our current circumstances and the possibility of whether there was even going to be a day after tomorrow.

It was here that I had my first taste of the local firewater, Calvados. We'd called out to an elderly French farmer, as we lay along a hedgerow awaiting the order to move off into a small early-morning company attack. We thought we'd better warn him that he was approaching almost certain death if he continued to move towards an area that was soon to be rocketed by RAF Typhoons.

He seemed very reluctant to disclose what was in the small keg he carried in an unusual looking wheelbarrow. We managed to quietly entice him around to our side of the hedgerow, making sure we didn't attract the attention of the enemy. He could only understand a little English so we decided to check the keg out for ourselves.

It wasn't long before enamel mugs were being removed from our small packs, as the well-preserved farmer uneasily nodded us an assurance that it was all right for us to drink. At the same time he was also giving unmistakeable indications that he wasn't eager to part with too much of it. Some of our platoon mates were a little wary, as there'd been rumours of Canadian soldiers dying after mistakenly drinking rocket fuel. Only a few of us were game enough to drink more than half a mug of the throat-burning spirit that to me seemed like a gift from the gods, coming when it did.

Not long after, I vaguely remember our platoon sergeant passing word along the hedgerow for bayonets to be fixed, and almost simultaneously we heard the sound of aircraft rapidly losing height as they screamed into a dive towards our objective, heralding the opening of our company attack. This turned out to be the only time in Normandy when I'd not felt apprehensive as I was leaving the start line for an attack. For that reason alone I'll never forget my introduction to Calvados.

Machine gun and mortar fire forced our platoon to go to ground several times as we made our way up a lightly timbered gradual incline. I can remember leaning against a tree that was growing at the edge of a small duck pond cut into the slope, just as a mortar bomb exploded among a flock of geese only yards away. It left me spattered with blood amidst a fallout of feathers and screeching birds. A piece of bark about as big as my hand suddenly disappeared from the tree only inches from my head. The sound and sight of this had a sobering effect. I literally came quickly down to earth again.

Our platoon commander by this time had begun shouting abuse at me from forty yards away. It seemed that in my more than slightly inebriated state I was the only one in the platoon who didn't think it was necessary to take cover. As more bombs sent shrapnel churning up the calm water of the pond, I was actually laughing according to our sergeant. My first encounter with Calvados had left me with a lot of explaining to do before the day was out.

Later that morning, after occupying a group of farms towards the top of the slope, we found all but about a dozen or so of the enemy had been able to evacuate our objective. There had been very little opposition.

After only a few short exchanges of rifle and machine gun fire, a small number of grubby looking German soldiers decided to vacate their isolated farm buildings and trenches before raising their hands above their heads. One claimed he was a stretcher-bearer but he'd been caught adorning his chest with a Red Cross shield. But it was obvious that he'd just crawled away from the deviously positioned Spandau he'd been manning.

Others who'd tried to remain in hiding among damaged buildings were eventually flushed from their cover with phosphorous grenades, one of which must have fallen into straw, creating a fire in one of the biggest of the buildings.

Then, following a few more bursts of Sten and rifle fire, the remaining Germans quickly discarded their weapons. Surprisingly, some of them looked relieved and seemed happy to become prisoners. Could this be a sign of better days ahead?

Then, quite unexpectedly, an enemy soldier emerged from one of the outer buildings and tried to ride off on a motorbike just as we were about to start digging in about a hundred yards away. We waved and shouted for him to stop but he either ignored or wasn't aware of our warning and tried to escape at high speed. He was later gunned down by men of another platoon.

I'm sure no one in B Company got any satisfaction from this, just the opposite in fact. But they'd been left with no option. He'd been a despatch rider and when checked out, his heavy leather satchel was found to contain a considerable amount of German-French occupational currency.

Although enemy shelling was increasing and we still had our own trenches to complete, within an hour the German despatch rider had been buried in a temporary shallow grave at the roadside, the grave clearly marked to make sure it would be attended to later. Our claim to a share of the booty he'd been carrying was conveniently ignored by our platoon commander.

The bodies of three or four unfortunate elderly French farmers were lying along a stone wall about thirty yards away from the trench that I was digging, and there was at least one woman among them. Rocket-firing Typhoons had struck so unexpectedly, the farmers had been unable to get away to safety.

Not long after we'd consolidated the area, the batman to our platoon commander, Lieutenant Elwood, was killed. It happened while they were doing a local reconnaissance, a little less than a hundred yards in front of our newly-won position. The batman had made the mistake of walking through a small gap in a hedgerow that concealed a German S-mine.

Lieutenant Elwood suspected a trap and shouted a warning, but just a split second too late to save the batman.

He'd been the only casualty in our platoon for the past two days. Lieutenant Elwood was very upset over his death. They'd been together for a long time, since well before the landings I was told. His replacement, Private Coffey, like the lieutenant and several others in our platoon, had been part of the initial beach group on D-Day. All of them had been members of the King's Liverpool Regiment before joining 8th Brigade as reinforcements days after the Normandy landings.

The previous afternoon, we'd come close to disaster when we attempted to capture a particular objective. We were supposed to get supporting fire from an American artillery unit that was in a position a few miles away to the north-west of us. Just after we'd begun leaving the start line, huge shells came crashing down a little more than two hundred yards or so in front of us, and in seconds completely wiped out a small Friesian dairy herd that we'd been preparing to pass through.

We continued to move forward in extended order while anxiously awaiting someone to call a halt to our advance. Then, just when a catastrophe looked imminent, and without receiving any orders, we all turned about and ran, sprinting for a couple of hundred yards in complete disarray, back to beyond our original start line.

I can remember finishing up in a small quarry where a couple of British officers were desperately trying to make radio contact in a bid to clarify the situation. Several men in our company had become battle casualties. There was uncertainty as to who was responsible for the shelling. The afternoon attack was aborted until the following morning, when we would have the support of the RAF Typhoons.

On the grapevine, we heard that the shelling had been by the Americans who had offered to support us with artillery from several miles away. Their guns were a few hundred yards off target, probably because of an incorrect map reference. Had we moved from the start line a few seconds sooner I'm sure we'd have lost at least half of B Company that afternoon.

Two days later, we carried out a part-battalion attack on a small rocky hilltop at the end of a long spur that our spotter aircraft had reported was fortified by German troops. For this offensive, we had the support of our own divisional 25-pounders that had caught up with us at last, following our speedy advance into lightly timbered, undulating farmland. A little more than forty minutes into this attack all enemy resistance on the hilltop had been silenced. We occupied the German positions without too many shots being fired.

Our artillery had literally torn their defences apart, shells detonating on the rocky ground which increased their effectiveness. This attack was carried out in a copybook-like manner, similar to the way in which the BEF had been routed in May of 1940 by the then all-conquering Wehrmacht. Today the situation had been in complete reverse. The Germans were no longer being matched against ill-equipped and poorly-trained troops with no support. We were lucky to have our artillery support us in this attack.

Now that the tide was beginning to turn, I couldn't help feeling a little sorry for the hapless enemy. The Germans left behind many dead. I remember the sorrowful sight of a couple of severely shell-shocked German soldiers wandering hopelessly around their unattended rocky, out-cropped and lightly timbered positions. They were too far gone to realise what had happened.

About fifteen badly-wounded German infantrymen lay scattered in and around their trenches, nearly all of them stretcher cases. Several had stomach wounds and very likely would not survive the day. Our officers radioed for field ambulances to be sent forward urgently. It wasn't long before several Red Cross jeeps were cautiously making their way up the hillside. The worst of the wounded were evacuated. While assisting with enemy-wounded, I saw how skilfully the Germans had prepared their hilltop positions. The only approach had been across a wide stretch of open ground.

Our intelligence section had got it right this time, because without the 25-pounders our company could well have been massacred. Scattered here and there around the German positions were many Scotch whisky bottles and the remains of some British compo rations and cigarettes. This finally solved the mystery surrounding the disappearance of one of our Bren gun carriers and its cargo that went missing thirty-six hours earlier. Many of these enemy soldiers may well have fought their last battle with smiles on their faces, given the empty bottles that were strewn in and around their trenches. Our artillery bombardment might well have interrupted a wild drinking session.

We'd been gradually closing the gap towards the town of Flers. Within an hour, German shells began crashing down along the spur, not much more than seventy or eighty yards from their old positions. Enemy gunners had begun ranging in, unaware or unconcerned about the plight of their wounded comrades. The shelling brought with it the order for our company to continue the advance.

We moved quickly, jogging our way down the rugged enemy-side of the hill beneath the screech of incoming German shells. We overran more enemy trenches that appeared to have been hastily evacuated about two hundred yards further on. From one of these trenches, I risked the consequences of a booby trap and picked up a German sniper rifle, only to find that its former handler had damaged the scope. We kept moving in the general direction of enemy guns, slowed down at times by machine gun fire. Though the gunfire was heavy, the guns seemed to be firing indiscriminately, so thankfully there were no casualties.

German troops were surrendering in larger numbers. On several occasions, I'd been detailed to escort about a dozen German prisoners back to our temporary divisional POW cage. Most of us found this duty a welcome break from the frontline. Taking prisoners to the POW cage was like getting a short leave pass. It could be a steady stroll, or at times a preferred dawdle. We could sometimes get as far back to our medium guns a few miles behind the line.

One time, a mate and I were about a mile behind the line with a group of prisoners, when we were forced to take cover in a ditch until enemy shelling eased. One of the prisoners, not overly concerned about the shelling, took a lump of black rye bread from his small haversack. I'm not sure if it was because I hadn't tasted bread in months since landing in Normandy, but the German must have noticed me staring at his bread. He promptly offered me a piece. Another German prisoner, a somewhat over-zealous young SS officer, muttered something to the contrary. He had a nasty leg wound and while we had been making our way from the line, his fellow prisoners had to take turns to help him walk. But I noticed, because of the officer's typical SS arrogance, some of them had done so with reluctance.

Perhaps, it was curiosity or just to remind the brazen SS officer that he was a prisoner and the war was now over for him that I accepted the offer. The bread, though a bit tough, tasted all right. To this day, when sinking my teeth into a piece of dark rye pumpernickel, my thoughts wander back to that war-embattled ditch in Normandy and the defiant German prisoner who'd introduced me to it.

When the prisoners first made contact with us, their immediate concern must have been what kind of treatment would be meted out to them. Some looked at us as though they were expecting to be lined up and shot. By the time we got to the cage, although exhausted and dejected, they looked more at ease as they realised they would now most likely survive the war. That same concern was occupying the minds of countless others. Men in our own division had also been showing signs of fatigue, especially those ever-diminishing numbers of men who'd been among the first to hit Sword Beach on D-Day. But since the fighting on the western side of the bridgehead was proving to be easier, they were inspired to "soldier on".

The fighting continued more or less the same, over the next few weeks and any man who carried a rifle and bayonet, if given an opportunity to put pen to paper, could quickly fill a book with his experiences.

There were encouraging signs that the Normandy campaign was slowly drawing to its inevitable conclusion. During one of the quieter moments, I was offered the opportunity to become a member of the brigade's exclusive Sniper Wing. At that time, the Wing was part of 8th Infantry Brigade's intelligence section, a small select group, which had been the pride and joy of Brigadier E. E. E. Cass. The Sniper Wing had unfortunately lost many of its numbers within the first couple of weeks of the landings, so, when the call came for replacements I decided I should give it a go. I knew that I'd proven my ability with a rifle, and I thought it would be a bit of a challenge. With those sentiments in mind, I'd decided to put my name down and take a few fairly simple aptitude tests.

I thought that, as a sniper, there'd be a more specific role for me, rather than being just an also-ran in the infantry. I knew I was an above average shot and I also had a natural flair to quickly disappear into the landscape, something I'd learned in the countryside near Birmingham during my not-all-that-long-ago childhood. Sniping was unquestionably riskier than being in the infantry, because you had to spend a lot more time in close proximity to the enemy. However, it offered me a way to use more of my own initiative.

Later, my shooting capability was put to the test under the watchful eye, as chance had it, of Brigadier Cass himself. He was a top marksman who had competed in the army's "Best Hundred Shots" for many years. I also learned I'd scored above average in the various other tests. So, I became a sniper, replacing a chap who had been very well-liked and an exceptionally good sniper.

The role of a sniper in 8th Brigade usually meant spending most daylight hours deployed in No Man's Land, close to or within enemy lines, depending on the type of terrain. Our main purpose was to seek out information for divisional and brigade intelligence. It was a lot less sinister than the name suggested. Snuffing out lives of ordinary enemy soldiers wasn't our top priority. We didn't want to give the enemy the slightest inkling of our presence in any particular section of the line.

Although the topic was never discussed, it was taken for granted that enemy scalps at this point in time would not get us any sooner to the Siegfried Line. We always had our personal sniper rifle at hand, with no more than five rounds of ammo, which we hoped we'd still have when we returned to our lines just after dark. After a few assignments we seemed to develop a strong attachment to our weapon, in my case, a Mark 4 Lee-Enfield sniper rifle that was married to a 32Mk 2 Telescopic-sight.

This type of sniping was carried out along similar lines to what is known in the army as a Standing or Listening Patrol. Usually we'd go forward with a companion, our dress mainly a camouflaged smock and face-veil. Snipers had to be proficient in field-craft, especially in Normandy, if we were to survive.

We were soon aware we were matching our wits against an experienced and most highly-trained, ruthless enemy. There were times when we'd be called upon to take an artillery observer forward with us, or sometimes a Typhoon pilot. Generally before an attack, one of our own officers might leave our lines and come with us to get a closer view of enemy positions. Only a few weeks into the Normandy campaign, the practice of sending snipers along with leading units when going into attacks was discontinued by 8th Brigade because the high casualty rate made it almost impossible to find suitable sniper replacements.

One of the toughest assignments was dealing with enemy snipers. These were sometimes ordinary German riflemen who'd been cunningly deployed to stir up trouble within our forward units that were holding the line. In early October, 1944, in one of the easier yet still cagey assignments, a mate, Eric Dutton, and I were near the small Dutch township of Overloon during 3rd Division's push towards Venray. The request for our services had come from a unit of the 1st Battalion, the King's Own Scottish Borderers, who were in 9th Brigade, which put added pressure on us to perform well.

How we came to get the task was a bit of a mystery because the KOSBs had their own snipers. We thought it must have been because of their close proximity, as well as the awkwardness of access to their exposed and isolated position.

On the other hand, the decision may well have been a less than considered gesture, by the flamboyant Brigadier Cass, made while he'd been entertaining senior officer friends for drinks.

Anyway, to get to the unit that required our services, we had to take the risk and cross exposed, open fields. Soon after we started, we came under sporadic enemy small arms fire. We lay in a shallow open drain in freezing conditions while we questioned our options. We still hadn't established exactly where we were, and the wide featureless, flat terrain rendered military maps more or less useless. We could see a prominent mound about three or four hundred yards away in the general direction where we had to go, and figured it might provide us with some sort of cover.

Once again, we came under irritating rifle fire as we made our way towards the mound, crossing old cultivations that because of their bareness and the prevalent icy conditions, could easily have been somewhere in Ukraine in the late autumn. Adding to the torment was the occasional nagging crack and whine from enemy bullets displacing crisp air as they streaked by. But as marksmen, we considered we'd have to be extremely unlucky to be hit from that distance. For all the discomfort they were causing us and our somewhat fugitive-like situation, we had an important detail to carry out and we just had to get on with it.

After much cursing and a lot of frowning, we made it to the mound. It was about twenty feet long and roughly two feet high, and covered by tarpaulins. It was positioned at the edge of a wide, shallow spoon drain that stretched a fair distance between large, bare cultivations.

Because we were still being subjected to intermittent rifle fire, we decided to take a breather for a few minutes. Before moving on again we curiously lifted a corner of a tarpaulin and were shocked at what was underneath. The mound where we had laid beside for cover contained the near-frozen corpses of about twenty British soldiers. We also saw that the insignia on some of their khaki tallied with that of the unit we were trying to reach.

We managed to make contact with the unit half an hour later. The small section of the KOSBs were occupying the northernmost tip of a long, narrow stand of pine trees, forty yards wide and stretching for many hundreds of yards. It was most likely a windbreak for crops. Some men of the unit were occupying the loft of a small farmhouse, just inside the pines.

The loft provided us with a view of the reported danger zone including a hay-stack about seventy yards away in the corner of a small stockyard. Beyond was an area that was lightly timbered. Its canopy spread over thick undergrowth which extended as far as the eye could see and no doubt could provide good natural cover for enemy snipers.

Patrols hadn't been commissioned yet to check out the area. So, there was uncertainty about the actual location and strength of enemy forward positions. I distinctly remember I could get an excellent view from the farmhouse loft by simply but cunningly inserting a small apple to separate roofing tiles, providing me with a visor. Our task was made easier by the KOSB's CSM who seemed keen, energetic and very obliging. He had done much of the required field investigation himself before we arrived.

After a few hours, my sniper mate and I were able to very cautiously move through and check out what the CSM had described as the "dark area". He was concerned about an area roughly around five hundred yards long, where he thought enemy riflemen had been laying out. He was worried they could move up close without being detected under the thick cover.

We then suggested a couple of ways to help, since with the oncoming winter, the KOSBs could be occupying this location for quite some time. We suggested a listening patrol should be placed at least a hundred yards out into the area, and should be occupied during all daylight hours.

We also recommended that trip-flares be placed in selected positions as there didn't seem to be any stray livestock around to trigger them off. These trip-flares could give early warnings of possible enemy encroachments under cover of darkness.

The CSM, along with a couple of his sergeants, thanked us for our services over a mug of tea and a chat. They'd obviously felt more at ease after seeing us move through the dense landscape that they'd believed was a haven for snipers and from where they reckoned they'd been repeatedly fired from.

We didn't mention to them that we were both sure it hadn't been enemy snipers. Like us, the German snipers would have been trained not to waste ammunition and disclose their presence unnecessarily. It wasn't long before light began to fade, making our return journey a lot more comfortable than the trip out. And we hadn't disappointed Brigadier Cass.

After almost two months in my new role, I had a welcome break from the fighting to attend 3rd Division's Sniper School in the Dutch town of Helmond, about twenty miles behind the line. The course was interesting, very beneficial and, with the approaching winter in mind, designed to prepare us for sniping in defence, as against our recent roles in attack. For the first time in many months, I was beyond the range of German mortars, making it easier to get a decent night's sleep.

It only lasted a week, but for that time there had been no one to wake me at a ridiculously early hour to make sure I'd be positioned somewhere out in No Man's Land before daybreak, where, with my fingers crossed, I hoped there'd be no clashes with German patrols along the way, before I settled into the landscape.

The half hour or so before dawn and our departure from the forward trenches were the most uneasy parts of the day for a sniper, a time when we were more vulnerable, a time when the predator could easily become the prey.

In fact, one such incident cost us a couple of men in an ambush out from Venray. It was now early December, and very cold. I'd just celebrated my nineteenth birthday with a dinner of bully beef, washed down by an extra special rum ration that my fellow snipers had somehow managed to deviously procure. At that time, I shared a small trench in deep snow with two mates, snipers Eric Dutton and John Coady. This particular trench was positioned at the end of a long, shallow communication trench which recently received a near direct hit from a mortar as we were enjoying one of our keenly contested nightly games of cribbage.

Luckily, the Royal Ulster Rifles who had had the trench before us, had placed a few layers of thin pine logs beneath several feet of heaped-up earth to make the small sleeping section close to mortar proof. Needless to say, our cribbage game had been called off early that night. The trench was in a small clearing just inside the edge of a semi mature pine plantation close to temporary battalion headquarters, and about a mile or so north-west of the Dutch town of Venray.

We were aware a German surveillance aircraft had been photographing our positions around midnight, a couple of nights earlier, so it was of no surprise that their mortaring was spot on. Several bombs straddled our isolated group of trenches and wrote off a jeep and trailer parked about thirty feet away. While occupying that particular position, it came as a bit of a morale booster to hear huge enemy shells screaming overhead at regular intervals, sounding like fighter aircraft diving, before detonating several miles behind our lines. These shells were most likely being fired from the west wall of the Siegfried Line, which was after all these years, not that many miles away, albeit on the other side of the River Maas.

Snow and the bitterly cold weather during recent weeks had restricted both sides to mainly patrol activity. Our patrols were mostly seeking information, but the Germans had sent in fighting patrols or raiding parties, some of them a hundred men strong. An encounter with one of these enemy fighting patrols resulted in me losing good mates near the Dutch village of Wanssum. This engagement may well have been timed with many others to coincide with the beginning of their unsuccessful mid-December offensive against the Americans in the Ardennes.

Lying out in crisp snow was a new skill to be mastered by the men of the Sniper Wing, despite the snowsuits that we'd urgently requested not arriving up the line until a week or so after the thaw. During the months of December, January, and early February, most of 3rd Division was sparsely spread along the River Maas in the Venray sector.

Towards the end of December, we watched inquisitively as our armoured support was stealthily taken out of the line, under cover of Bofors fire. A number of guns were brought in very close to our trenches at various points along the line to fire low air bursts across enemy positions. This made them keep their heads down and helped muffle the movement of the departing tanks.

We learned the armoured division was destined to go back into Belgium to assist the Americans who were reeling following the huge unexpected German counter offensive towards Bastogne, a hundred miles or so to the south. While waiting for the spring offensive, the battalions of 3rd Division were spending twenty days in and ten days out of our forward trenches.

Our closeness to enemy-held positions prevented excessive mortaring and shelling up front. As often the case in Normandy, our forward trenches were sometimes more reposeful than the ones we occupied during our ten days in reserve. Most battalions were taking it easy, a few men even managing to visit a mobile shower unit. For most of them it was the first time they'd been able to get their louse-ridden clobber off since leaving England six months before.

However, there wasn't any respite for the men of Sniper Wing. For us, the latter day Paul Reveres of the British Army, it remained business as usual. Some of us were also plagued with lice, but it was still necessary for someone to keep the enemy under surveillance.

By the time we'd reached the banks of the Rhine, many units were experiencing a slow but sure decline in morale. This was more evident within divisions that had fought their way right through from El Alamein. Recent news-sheets had led us to believe our Russian allies were moving doggedly towards Berlin, arousing wishful thinking that the war might end abruptly.

We could sense new feelings of apprehension within the platoons. What if I should become a casualty just days before this long-drawn-out war reaches its conclusion? Many of these fellows had been slogging it out, on and off for more than five years. It was hard enough for single men, but for married men with children it must have been a real mind-tester.

Chapter Nine: And Into Germany

At last, we sensed the war in Europe was entering its final stages. For many of the men who served in rifle companies, along with our close colleagues who provided us with armoured support, to have survived through to Germany was, for a lot of them, more than they'd cared to think about. Many of these men hadn't even contemplated life after Normandy and I must admit to having been one of them. For some of the chaps in the battalion, the question had not been whether they'd be around to see the end of the war, but, rather, how soon their departure from the scene might be, and what form it would take.

It was customary and accepted as part of an infantryman's lot to complain. But for all our whingeing and our regular expressions of dissatisfaction, there was always an equivalent amount of spontaneous good humour and laughter in our platoons. Much of the humour must have been subconsciously influenced from the knowledge that, unlike a few of our old trench-sharing mates, at least we were still around and kicking.

This grim form of jocularity was particularly noticeable after having come safely through the most recent attack. Laughter also helped ward off fear that most of us felt, particularly when we were continually getting what we thought was the lion's share of the fighting. Good humour would be evident as we'd dig our latest slit trench right up until we were briefed about our next objective and the scale of the coming attack. Then a more sober mood would set in, with stress and fatigue again apparent on the faces of a lot of young but battle-weary men; young men who seemed to have aged several years in just six months.

We were participating in a very serious on-going game of "Russian Roulette", and it was definitely not everyone's cup of tea. Surprisingly, the platoon's morale seemed to be reasonably high. The fact that the Allies controlled the sky must have had a big influence on that. Even back in Normandy, morale had been pretty good, especially when taking into account the bitter stalemate that had existed for the weeks following the landings, and the high casualties and discomforts. Before the landings, few expected the months ahead would be easy. I'm sure the majority of Monty's young frontline soldiers had been secretly preparing for the worst.

Now, a little more than nine months later, we were relaxing near our trenches as we watched convoys of huge road-transports bringing forward assault boats and pontoon bridging equipment. Their loads were being stockpiled around hillsides only a few miles from our current positions in preparation for the inevitable attack across the Rhine.

Unlike their pivotal role in D-Day, 3rd Division was spared the task of spearheading the offensive into Germany through the Reichswald forests. There was an air of excitement when we crossed the border into Germany, perhaps because the outbreak of the war had been so long ago. So many had suffered for us to get this far. So much had happened since those unpredictable months of 1939.

I remembered the day gas masks had been distributed at my school, and we were told, 'Don't worry, boys and girls, the Germans will never be game enough to make us use them.'

It brought much laughter and we all thought it a little funny when our teachers told us to walk around the playground a couple of times in our masks, just to make sure no one had any problems. I also recalled those long cold nights five years ago when I'd helped my mother into that water-logged air raid shelter in our back yard, often after she'd spent half the day in a food queue. I thought about those mornings on the bus after a night in the shelter, when we'd learn from fellow passengers about friends or neighbours who had become overnight casualties. If we could only survive the next few weeks we might yet experience the dream of the late Neville Chamberlain, our ex Prime Minister and fellow Brummie. Almost seven years earlier he'd returned from Munich promising us "Peace in our time".

During the last couple of weeks, many platoons took it on themselves to rename the BLA. We'd been fighting under the "British Liberation Army" title since June 6, 1944. But, for most of Montgomery's younger soldiers, BLA now clearly read: "Burma Looms Ahead". This unofficial new title was especially popular with the eighteen and nineteen-year olds, many of whom had been in uniform for less than twelve months.

It wasn't hard to imagine they were destined to go to Burma as soon as the Germans were defeated. Our feelings regarding the Japanese Army were very different to how we regarded the Germans. British soldiers were well aware of the dreadful atrocities committed by ruthless Japanese forces in China and indeed all around the Pacific. Their brutality was well documented. The feeling among some British soldiers was that, although the Germans were a formidable foe, on rare occasions they had shown us a degree of mutual soldierly respect.

I'd witnessed an example of what set them apart from the Japanese in mid September, soon after we'd moved on from Normandy.

My company had been selected to create a diversion to dupe the enemy into thinking 8th Brigade was about to make a major crossing of the Escaut Canal, two or three miles from the small Dutch town of Weert. Unfortunately for me, the very under-strength B Company had been selected to act as a decoy to draw enemy fire in a bid to assist 8th Brigade to achieve a surprise crossing of the canal several miles away.

My company was offloaded from trucks into woodland that was separated from the canal by about five hundred yards of bare cultivations extending to the foot of the fairly steep canal bank. From there we could look out over roof tops of houses and over a prominent church spire in Weert. Along with about nine others from my platoon, we were sent out to investigate the canal bank, knowing that there was a good possibility we'd also make contact with the enemy.

As expected, we were soon fired upon. Lt John Elwood who led the patrol was very lucky to have survived a bullet in the head as we attempted to make our way up the slope of the canal bank. We managed to crawl three hundred yards under all kinds of small arms fire along a shallow drainage trench that ran along farmland to a small clump of trees. We finally got to our lines by way of a small stream that meandered right back into our woodland positions. It was miraculous that there were no further casualties.

The strategists at Battalion Headquarters then decided that my platoon should step up the diversion by occupying part of the canal bank closest to us, which we did under the cover of a barrage from our divisional 25-pounders while experiencing heavy enemy machine gun fire.

After laying out along the sheltered side of the canal's tow-path for another 24 hours under constant machine gun fire, Brigade HQ then decided we still weren't attracting enough enemy attention.

So, they decided to send assault boats forward under cover of darkness that night, in readiness for the platoon that had been held in reserve to attempt a dawn crossing of the canal.

As a result, almost all the men in one of B Company's platoons, my old platoon, were either killed or wounded. The couple of men who survived were calling for help as they lay wounded on the canal's tow-path under constant heavy machine gun fire.

The ferocity of close-up enemy fire power confronting B Company made it obvious that our small but vital role in the brigade strategy should have been temporarily aborted. It had been an unnecessary suicidal attempt to cross the canal. Had it been aborted, we could have fallen back a couple of hundred yards, allowing our divisional artillery, already ranged in on the enemy's position, to soften up the Germans without compromising the task that B Company had been given.

While trying to aid the wounded, our company stretcher-bearer decided he'd have to take risks, and this he did by hanging his clearly marked Red Cross satchel on the end of a stretcher before waving it just below the top of the canal bank. Because of the accuracy and overwhelming intensity of superior fire power from enemy machine guns, anyone raising his head above the top of the canal bank would become an instant casualty.

I was only thirty feet away from the stretcher-bearer, where I'd been lying alongside a Bren gun, having failed, with other Bren gunners, to give supporting fire to our mates as they'd tried with little success to cross the canal.

It had taken just about a minute-and-a-half for us to lose the battle of fire-power against the much faster firing Spandaus that had been laying in wait, firing from well-prepared, concealed positions in undergrowth forty or fifty yards away on the opposite side of the canal.

Exactly as my former platoon commander had forewarned, the Germans had cleverly waited until our small assault boats were mid-way across the narrow canal before resuming heavy fire, killing most of the entire platoon in just a couple of minutes. They must have thought we were stupid to have attempted such an idiotic, untenable mission.

During the continuing exchange of fire, a minute or so later, I saw that one of my mates, Private Carol, had been hit. He, like me, was one of six temporary Bren gunners who'd been selected specifically for this operation. He was lying two or three feet away. Although he was obviously suffering from shock, he didn't look particularly worried when he yelled out to me that he thought he'd finally got a "Blighty".

Carol, a lightly-built fellow who wore spectacles, had received two bullet wounds, one in his left shoulder, and one that he was unaware of, that had pierced his helmet. The bullet had removed a narrow strip of skin and hair from his scalp. Seconds later, after another burst of Spandau fire, I felt sure that I'd also been hit when I felt a solid whack near my nose and blood began to drip over the butt of my Bren gun.

After getting through just two magazines, I took my finger off the trigger momentarily and was relieved to find that, though my face was covered in blood, the damage was superficial. I had a laceration above my lip. I'd been hit with either dislodged debris from the canal's gravelled tow-path, or by a fragment from a ricochet.

I helped Carol the few feet down the slope of the lightly timbered canal bank. Then as I attended his shoulder wound, blood began to dribble across his forehead. Though his scalp had been grazed he could get around unaided. He actually shouted across to Lieutenant Elwood, saying that since our stretcher-bearer was preoccupied tending to the wounded spread along the tow-path, he would make his own way back to our Company's temporary lines on the edge of woodlands, four or five hundred yards away.

I returned to near the top of the canal bank in time to see the stretcher being raised. I was amazed to see it as I'd been expecting it would be shot to pieces.

The German soldiers directly facing us had held their fire so we could tend to our wounded. They had been shot down at point blank range while attempting to get three or four assault boats into the canal. Without immediate assistance they would most likely have died from their wounds.

We were all very much aware that, unlike the Germans, the Japanese didn't subscribe to any kind of chivalry. This was why Burma, in the eyes of most British soldiers, was such a frightening prospect.

About twenty young men from my old platoon had been killed in that terrible exercise in stupidity. Our company had creditably carried out its task that morning, but at a ridiculous cost. We were exhausted. Just before arriving back at our woodland positions, we were met by B Company's quartermaster.

He seldom got too close to the action and jovially promised each of us a new pair of socks as though he was giving us the world. I thought this unusual offer indicated the kind of value they now put on our lives. A double-rum ration would have been better after what we'd experienced during the past forty-eight hours. The QM was hurt by our pithy response as he thought he was being generous. Was he expecting us all to break into song at this rare little gesture he'd made?

I couldn't help feeling that the men in my old platoon, many of whom I'd spent most of my time with in Normandy, were sent to their deaths unnecessarily. In fact, my feelings were that the whole exercise and its successful outcome appeared to have had little strategic gain. It was more than likely carried out simply as an alternative measure, perhaps an excuse to get 8th Brigade off the over-congested road heading north towards Arnhem.

Later that year, our stretcher-bearer was awarded a military medal for this and several other similar acts under fire.

The ill-fated platoon's commander was a Canadian lieutenant who, apart from being a very popular fellow, was also a top soldier. I can remember on one occasion during the early days of the Normandy fighting when he was my platoon's commander, that he led a night patrol that brought back two German soldiers for interrogation to our trenches. He was lucky. I could have very easily shot him on his return to our lines about 2 a.m.

Communications being what they were, I hadn't been warned he was out in front. His three-man patrol plus two grubby looking and very strong German infantrymen, reeking of Bulgarian tobacco, came in right at my trench, where they'd been roughly frisked before being taken away for interrogation.

On the day of the Escaut Canal massacre, about an hour before daybreak, I'd spoken with my former platoon commander as we crouched near the top of the canal bank, while watching men from one of B Company's other platoons quietly dragging canvas assault boats forward, under cover of darkness. The Canadian lieutenant had told me he thought his platoon was about to be massacred. His prediction sadly proved to be true, as with the breaking of dawn came the near annihilation of his platoon. The order to cross the canal without sufficient covering fire was ridiculous.

We all knew it wasn't necessary to actually cross the canal to draw concentrated enemy fire. We had already experienced constant, heavy enemy machine gun fire since we'd positioned ourselves along the canal, some thirty-six hours earlier.

This operation must have been planned by senior officers miles away from the scene of the action, and ignorant as to what the situation required. We could only assume the old 1914-18 die-hards back at Brigade HQ were still entertaining traits of attrition.

Their antiquated battle strategies held little thought for the lives of the young men they'd turned their backs on. This was despite being made aware that reinforcements were unlikely to be forthcoming.

Had this incident occurred a few weeks earlier in Normandy, where most of our actions were on a brigade or divisional scale, I might have been less critical despite the fighting being more vicious and the casualties greater.

To gain territory, we knew we had to be prepared to lose men. But to see soldiers shot down unnecessarily when it could so easily have been avoided, was tragic.

After being hit at very close range, several of our men had fallen into the canal from their small canvas boats and drowned. We had to listen to their calls for assistance above the sound of intense machine gun fire, and although some were less than twenty feet away from us, there was nothing we could do for them.

And so B Company 1st Battalion South Lancs, in just five days, had located and made contact with the enemy, before creating the required diversion that took the lives of at least twenty men.

It had been a costly, but successful diversion. 8th Brigade had taken more than four hundred German prisoners who'd been enticed by the diversion. One German prisoner told us that among three Allied prisoners they'd captured and managed to evacuate, was a Canadian officer. This, he said, had happened only an hour before the Germans had been completely encircled by the Allies. The battalions of 8th Brigade had fanned out behind them, following a relatively quiet crossing of the canal and the liberation of Weert a few miles away.

Next morning, I found out that about a dozen men of B Company had been given temporary graves on a vacant block between two small Dutch cottages, only a short distance from the canal where they'd been sacrificed. My old section leader, Corporal Spittle, was among them. He was someone who I'd felt deeply indebted to after he'd courageously come to my aid near the Normandy village of Banneville, some two months before.

He'd taken it upon himself to leave the safety of his trench and raced a hundred yards across open ground during enemy mortaring to help me. He got me out of a sticky situation that had arisen soon after he'd sent me to make contact with another of our platoons in an unfamiliar area. This platoon had been deployed just a few hours before in the edge of thick woodland, and close to where German positions were not well-defined. He'd thought I was about to walk blindly into German lines concealed by smoke and dust from enemy mortaring.

Also among the dead at the Escaut Canal was my mate, Private George Churchman. I'd got to know George very well when we'd shared many slit trenches together in Normandy, mainly around the time of our joining 8th Brigade and a week or so before and during Operation Goodwood. He was a lovely fellow, a Londoner from Walthamstow. On the odd occasion, he'd talked about his wife and the recent arrival of the first addition to his family, a toddler who would never get to see the dad who'd loved him so much.

This out-of-the-blue action had allowed 8th Brigade to isolate and take hundreds of enemy prisoners while surrounding and liberating the small Dutch town of Weert.

Twenty-four hours after digging temporary graves for our mates who were lost on the canal bank, we'd moved through Weert to be welcomed by most of the local population.

The soldiers' temporary graves were left covered with a carpet of flowers by Dutch civilians who'd arrived on the scene unexpectedly from out of nowhere to pay homage, many bringing along their children as they'd solemnly celebrated their first hours of liberation from the Germans.

Within twenty-four hours, we'd crossed the bridge into Weert to receive a gracious welcoming by most of the townspeople who'd lined the roadside, some of them actually warning us to be careful, yelling out to us that the Germans were not that far down the road. Our advance through Weert ended a couple of miles beyond the town after we came under minor sporadic machine gun fire. It was enough to make us fan out on both sides of the road and dig in to await the arrival of another unit that would take over from us, so that we could continue our journey north.

Soon, we were jockeying along with many other British units that were waiting to share the heavily congested road heading north towards Arnhem. Around mid-morning, we were surprised to see a couple of the enemy's new jet aircraft, our first sighting, go screaming a few hundred feet above the endless column slowly moving northwards.

The following day and night, we moved bumper to bumper in what seemed like an endless convoy of heavy troop transports and light armoured vehicles, at times along narrow and very exposed roads that the Dutch had constructed many years before. The roads were about ten to fifteen feet above the level of vast natural flood plains.

During the second night German anti-tank guns began taking their toll. The occasional truck that was hit became a fireball as most of them carried twenty or thirty jerry cans of additional fuel. These blazing vehicles were quickly manhandled and pushed down into the flood plain to keep the road open and the column moving.

Many casualties occurred and were laid out along the road's narrow and steep sloping verges, but, because of the inaccessibility of field ambulances due to the one-way traffic jammed road, the future of the casualties looked anything but bright. Though all of the twenty or so fellows sitting in the darkness at the back of our truck remained cautiously quiet throughout the ordeal, you could sense the relief each time we crawled past one of the blazing vehicles. They were aware that each time our track was illuminated by the flames, we were likely to become the next truck to be targeted.

After several hours of uneasiness, we finally got past that section of road which could only be described as a shooting gallery for the enemy.

Soon after daybreak, we caught up with the American 82nd Airborne Division and took over their trenches where they'd been dug in, just south of Nijmegen, near the small Dutch township of Grave. Despite being hungry and weary, these paratroopers had remained undaunted and welcomed us with smiles that showed exactly how happy they were to see us. They were just about out of rations and down to their last few rounds of ammunition. They even asked us for cigarettes, which was surprising to us, knowing that most Americans didn't care much for our smokes.

As we stood around their trenches waiting for them to get organised to leave, we jokingly asked an American platoon commander if he had faith in his anti-tank weapon that we could see covering the nearby lane. The lieutenant, eager to prove a point, promptly called out to "Tiger", his Bazooka operator, who fired a missile and quickly converted a steel garden shed into a heap of twisted metal. We all applauded. He certainly proved the accuracy of the weapon, but how effective it would be on an enemy tank left us deliberating.

While the changeover was taking place, the sky above filled with hundreds of the RAF's heavy bombers whose target was possibly Duisburg, as a huge pall of smoke was rising several thousand feet in that direction. German anti-aircraft shells were exploding above us and we saw at least two of the attacking Lancaster bombers nose-diving towards the ground before reaching their target. Some of the RAF crewmen appeared to be bailing out into German occupied territory.

There were some fellows in B Coy who thought it poetic justice, when a couple of weeks later, a certain senior officer of 8th Brigade had been mortally wounded near the Dutch town of Venray, a town just a few miles from the River Maas. Venray had been captured by our division as the first signs of the oncoming winter were beginning to appear.

We never really got to hear the full story about our tragic mission at the canal. Whether a misunderstanding, or a mistake, it was the result of questionable logic. Or perhaps it had been an exercise in applied lunacy, that was responsible for sending most of my old platoon mates to their doom, as they tried to accomplish a small but unnecessary dawn crossing of the Escaut Canal.

We were now in Germany, resting while occupying a position not far from the banks of the River Rhine, a few miles south-east of the German township of Calcar.

The 3rd Division's first big attack of the new year, had been an action that cleared an area roughly to the south-east of the heavily bombed town of Goch. The Allies were gradually closing towards the banks of the Rhine.

It was now early March, 1945. This was roughly the date I was to rejoin the South Staffordshires as I'd finally reached the Airborne Forces minimum required age of nineteen and a quarter. My old battalion had been severely depleted in late September, 1944, after a great many casualties in the battle for Arnhem and only remnants of the original battalion remained. It seemed unlikely my return to the Red Berets would go ahead immediately, as previously arranged.

Here, in our new position near the Rhine, when the wind was in a favourable direction, we could stretch out and even kick a ball around, while relaxing under cover of a smokescreen that was effectively provided by Canadian Army engineers.

At other times, we had to keep our heads down as we were exposed to enemy observation and plagued by sporadic shelling, shelling that was to cause us a few unexpected casualties before we were able to get moving again. Then, after hearing good news of the continuing Russian offensive towards Berlin, life in British infantry battalions which had seemed pretty cheap in recent times, was beginning to show signs of gaining some value.

It brought a smile to my face when I heard a couple of my sniper colleagues discussing football. They sounded more than just a little optimistic as they reminisced. In fact they were even talking of attending a Liverpool-Everton game in the not-too-distant future.

Two days earlier, a small group from Company HQ and a few others from around Battalion Headquarters, got a lecture from our regimental sergeant major, who'd taken it upon himself to try to whip up a bit of enthusiasm. We were to make our first major attack into Germany. He'd advised us that this attack would give us our first real opportunity to take out our revenge on the Germans for all the suffering they'd caused us and our families. Less than twenty-four hours later, 8th Brigade had overcome some reasonably stiff resistance before advancing several miles deeper into Germany.

I remember standing near a couple of farm buildings that just hours before we'd commandeered to use briefly as our headquarters. Near the wide-open doors of a well-kept barn, I watched men from our pioneer platoon as they applied a coat of white paint to a small heap of crosses, as an audience of half a dozen German children looked on. The crosses were to be placed on the temporary graves of the men who'd fallen during the morning's attack. I'd known at least two of them as they'd been lieutenants from my former company. Both had been excellent officers and, only a few months earlier, had nominated me to accompany them on one of their dreaded daylight patrols along the wooded banks of the River Mass. Night patrols were bad enough, but leaving our positions during the hours of daylight with each of these officers were times that most of us in B Coy had learned to hate.

Patrols with each of these iron-willed lieutenants were generally carried out under sufferance, directly accredited to their dedication. Both had set high standards by example and their loss was most tragic at this point in the war. But, as with many of their predecessors, after pushing their luck on so many occasions it had eventually forsaken them.

Moving into a small stock-yard around the other side of the barn, our RSM saw what he thought was some of our chaps taking out their revenge on a small assembly of Germans – some old men and a few women and children. The regimental sergeant major had been unable to hide a wry smile when he realised that the hapless Germans were actually being treated to chocolate, bully beef, cigarettes and soap. I'm sure this wasn't quite what he'd had in mind a couple of days before when he'd lectured us about the coming of "pay-back-time". To me, it just highlighted the stupidity of war. These Germans had also suffered; it was hardly fraternisation.

The skies over the last few weeks had been alive with unopposed marauding Allied aircraft. The seemingly endless drone of British heavy bombers in large numbers crossed our battalion trenches a couple of hours after sunset most evenings, taking the war into the far distant corners of the Fatherland. There were now regular batches of tired and dejected enemy soldiers finding their way into our lines with hands above their heads, these forlorn figures in field-grey appearing to be a shadow of the once high and mighty swaggering stormtroopers of the Wehrmacht.

We were finding it hard to believe that this was the same German Army that had shown such great confidence and self-esteem right up until the battle for Stalingrad. For so long, most of them had been easily motivated to the metallic clatter of their superior heavy Panzas and self-propelled guns, and equally able to gloat the terrifying shrieks and moans that echoed the firing of their deadly Nebelwerfers.

But, after that thorough defeat by the Russians in Stalingrad, the Germans had been in steady decline. Thank goodness, they were now unable to perform anything like the Rommel inspired fighting force we'd come to grips with in Normandy, little more than six months ago.

Surely the war couldn't go on for much longer at this rate; these, the questionable mumblings of wishful thinkers around the platoons.

Even the Wehrmacht's occasional reconnaissance patrols, as well as their sometimes-irregular shelling and mortar stonks were now at an all time low. Our most recent battalion news-sheets cautiously informed us of the amazing achievements of Marshal Zhukov's huge Russian Armies that were advancing on Berlin. In response, many of my mates jubilantly asked, 'Why the hell don't the Germans just throw in the towel so that we can all go home?'

Then, within a few weeks, the unbelievable happened, something that for most Britons had seemed far too much to hope for, way back during those bleak dark days of 1940.

That song!

The one we all loved to sing but knew was really a wishful expression of fantasy, and was only ever sung in jest following the sombre return of the routed British Army from Dunkirk.

The song that was often sung humorously in pubs during the time of the Blitz and early war years, seldom failed to bring much laughter among the many realists.

There'd also been sad times though, times when the same song brought a few hidden tears, not least when heard being sung euphorically by children taking cover during air raids, coaxed along by their equally anxious parents when endeavouring to play down the horrors of nightly bombings.

Now it seemed that chorus, "Whether the weather may be wet or fine, we'll stroll along without a care", might soon become lost along with other wartime memories.

"The Washing" was, at last... "hanging out on the Siegfried Line".

In Europe, for the first time in more than six years, guns had fallen silent. That ridiculous killing game, the one where there weren't any winners, along with the hideous masquerade of Adolf Hitler, had finally ended.

Chapter Ten: New Horizons and Final Respects

Following the declaration of peace in Europe, I was able to enjoy a pleasant, cushy role with the occupation force in Germany for a short time, but, when the war in the Pacific ended suddenly, and much sooner than we'd all expected, the army quickly lost its appeal for me. There'd been many good times when I'd really enjoyed wearing khaki.

How could any young soldier ever forget the great comradeship? However, since I had no wish to become a member of a peacekeeping force and knew there was also a lot of catching up to be done, I used much the same zeal to get out of the army that, more than five years earlier, I'd used to get in.

There'd been occasions during the Blitz when I'd questioned how devastating air raids were likely to become before the morale of civilians would finally reach breaking point. Now, after looking over the ruins of Hamburg and other heavily bombed towns, it seemed the residents of many Germany cities had been pushed into going beyond that point. For all the horrible atrocities the Nazis committed since Hitler became their Fuhrer, one could now feel a little sympathetic towards the German people. Apart from most rural areas, Germany was in complete shambles.

Before being shipped back to England, I was detailed for an assignment a little more interesting than the administrative work I had been doing. Five of us were to escort the staff cars bringing the advance guard of the Women's Auxiliary Territorial Service from Brussels into Germany. The car in which I was to ride "shot-gun" left the Belgian capital after a short delay caused by one of the group of women officers. The captain stubbornly insisted that she sit in the front passenger seat, despite being advised by the corporal driver that I, as the armed escort, had to occupy that particular seat. After some minutes of deliberation, the captain was helped into reconsidering her decision by her colonel, who advised that she should sit in the back of the eight-seat staff car with her.

Once we were underway, the trip was quite pleasant. The passengers – a colonel, a captain, a warrant officer as well as their first and second drivers – had brought along a hamper of nicely prepared food. We stopped to picnic shortly after crossing the Rhine. The lunch would have been more palatable had it not been for the hundreds of refugees casting their weary eyes in our direction as we parked just off the roadside. Many of these unfortunates would not have had a decent meal for some time.

We passed cautiously through parts of what was left of the bombed town of Munster along roads that had only recently been opened up through rubble. We then headed northeast before moving on to the autobahn north of Bielefeld.

We were often forced to slow down, some roads being clogged by refugees as well as tired and weary German servicemen slowly making their way homewards among crowds of displaced persons. Many were going in the opposite direction, all-in-all a very depressing sight.

After a few short stops and a little sightseeing, we arrived at Herford, a small town that was soon to become one of the occupational force's future headquarters, as light was beginning to fade. The women officers, being a bit of a novelty in this area at that time, were given a warm reception. They'd arrived at one of the nicer parts of Germany, one of stately homes amidst ornately landscaped gardens containing a variety of neatly appointed trees.

It appeared to be one of the few areas that hadn't suffered any obvious war damage. The captain seemed all smiles for some unknown reason before telling me she'd stuck her neck out to get permission for me to remain their escort for at least one more day. This gave me more time with the younger second driver, which was spent souvenir hunting among other things, while mooching nearby vacant homes that we'd been told, until recently, had been occupied by prominent Nazis.

The next day, one of the nicest assignments I'd ever undertaken came to an end. The young driver and I had started to become more than a little friendly, so perhaps it was just as well. I returned to my unit hoping to get wind of my demob date, secretly wishing my name would be mentioned among the next batch to head for home.

Certain incidents, amongst them the stupid unnecessary sacrifice of so many of my mates that fateful morning on the Escaut Canal, had been a real eye-opener for me; even though that particular action, from the army's point of view, had been a small operation. That, and a few other lesser acts of dubious rationality, left me with a strong desire to do my own decision making in the future, now that it looked like there was going to be a future.

I remembered only too well the remarks of Staff Sergeant Coombes way back at Lee-on-the-Solent during the Blitz, the day Eddie Atkinson died. He'd pointed out that, in the army, we were all just another bloody number. Although his words hadn't gone over too well at that time, after more than five years of saluting and heel-clicking, I was now beginning to realise he was probably right.

By November, 1945, many thousands of recently de-mobbed service personnel were once again walking the streets of Birmingham. I was still a teenager, but Joe Lake was experiencing a somewhat unusual kind of happiness to have just joined their ranks. It felt a little strange to be taking my first steps out of khaki, while the discarding of my heavy hobnailed boots left me with a gait that felt a little strange for a day or two.

I was now sporting a natty, fawn, double-breasted de-mob suit, which at that time was for me the first suit I'd ever possessed. But I was also very conscious of not having a job, and even worse, having no qualifications to help me get one. I was now a young adult civilian and in this role I felt very green, a rookie again, so to speak.

Apart from my very short-lived apprenticeship at Webley and Scott, my only recollection of civilian life was as a schoolboy.

Of all the many changes that had taken place since I left Brum, there was one that really struck me. For the first time, I was now legally old enough to walk into an English pub unaccompanied, and ask for a beer. As for the rest of it, I found my new life back in civvies was one where most things appeared as being trivial. It would have been very easy for me to go off the rails.

Out of khaki!

Nothing seemed to be all that important any more. Although I hadn't been aware of it until I'd been home a few months, I began to realise my nerves were in bad shape, making it easy for me to get into arguments and other awkward situations. It would take a couple of years before my better sense of reasoning returned. The time I'd spent in the army had been an education in itself, and I knew I would benefit from some aspects of it in one way or another for the rest of my life.

But it didn't take long to find there weren't any decent positions in the workforce for young unskilled men like me. This was one of the reasons I emigrated to Australia two years later after I successfully completed a returned serviceman's rehabilitation course in electronics.

I had many anxious moments however before I was accepted for the rehabilitation course. To begin with, I had to convince a selection panel that I'd never been a window cleaner, as was stated on my enlistment papers. They were adamant a window cleaner didn't have the required criteria for the high tech study in electronics and suggested I should try for a course in bricklaying or some other occupation with fewer technical requirements.

For a while, it looked as though the white lie I'd used to get into the army would now back-fire, preventing me from taking the training course of my choice. But after a couple of additional interviews and a lot of perseverance, the panel eventually decided to make an exception. Because I'd enlisted in the army during a time of emergency and at an early age, they decided to take a gamble with me; but only if I attended Suffolk Street Technical College three nights a week on top of spending five days each week at the training centre. They made it clear this would be necessary if I were to have any hope of satisfactorily completing the course.

The electronics course was not easy for me for two main reasons. Firstly, I'd had to start from scratch; whereas all the others in my class had already completed three or four years in the electronics industry before their enlistments. Secondly, my hearing problem had got progressively worse, due to an action that happened only months before the war ended,

A month or so before we got to Germany there'd been an incident in north eastern Holland. Up until then, I'd survived my service as a sniper right through to the Rhine, and been lucky to have escaped serious injury. We were not far from the German border during a quieter period in the fighting and occupied an isolated cottage that I'd been using for the surveillance of close-up enemy forward positions, mainly during the hours of daylight.

This particular cottage was about a hundred and fifty yards out from a small deserted township that was very close to known enemy lines and a little over half-a-mile or so in front of our own sparsely held positions.

My problem arose when I got an unscheduled daylight visit from a lieutenant, who, for no apparent reason, had stalked his way down from our forward positions. Later, I heard a theory that he'd possibly been looting. I remember feeling a little uneasy about his arrival, knowing quite well the cottage I was occupying would be under strict surveillance by the enemy.

Then, about half an hour after this officer had left to make his way back to our lines, I was beginning to think that perhaps I was taking my soldiering too seriously. I'd become a little battle weary and over-cautious. My concern over his visit was probably baseless. Even so, I was bewildered that he hadn't been fired on, when making his way in and out of several other isolated buildings a few hundred yards away.

My suspicions were realised afterwards when enemy guns began destroying my cottage observation post. The first shell screamed through the lower part of the roof opening up the ceiling just a couple of feet above my head, seconds before another slammed into the front of the cottage, noisily shattering a small section of brickwork a few feet below the upstairs window that I'd been observing from. Luckily, I was spared enough time to reach the back of the cottage to find some sort of cover before the next shells found their mark.

This situation was not entirely new to me as I'd experienced very similar circumstances, one of them only a matter of two weeks earlier. So, I was well aware of the drill needed to survive. But, in this instance, the accuracy of the initial shelling caught me unprepared. I was unable to take refuge in the cottage cellar, which I knew contained several feet of water.

I hugged the ground near some concrete steps at the rear of the small cottage which was little more than thirty or forty feet square, while shells appeared to be slowly reducing the building to rubble. As I lay there, I can remember feeling angry about the stupidity of the lieutenant who'd given away my position. But I was also considering myself lucky, realising that the enemy gunners only had armour-piercing ammunition. Had they been using high explosives, I'm pretty sure the war for me would have ended there and then.

After small pieces of the roof began falling on me, I could still exercise a certain degree of confidence working out intervals between shots. I dashed back up what remained of the cottage stairs to recover the field-phone that I'd hoped I could use to call on our own guns for support, or at least put our intelligence section into the picture as to what was happening.

Although I could see the phone was still intact, I couldn't use it; fallen masonry had buried the signal lines, making it impossible to drag the phone clear in the few seconds left before the next shells would hit.

To this day, I can still clearly recall the shock of seeing the destruction which had transformed that small quaint bedroom to a mass of broken timber and rubble. That cottage had provided me with a comfortable place to observe enemy positions for nearly two weeks. While counting the passing seconds, I must have subconsciously grabbed my scout-scope and compass from below the rubble before dashing back to the rear of the cottage. Time seemed to drag on and on before the shelling ceased.

I was told later that smoke was eventually put down by our 25-pounders allowing a patrol led by Lt. Carmichael to get me back to our lines. Luckily, I'd avoided being buried and received only superficial burns to my chest. My nose had also been badly bruised by falling masonry smashing into my face.

I spent the next few days on one of the many stretchers that littered the concrete floor of 8th Brigade's Casualty Clearing Station. Even today I can clearly remember the roofless convent that had been weather-proofed with tarpaulins, only a couple of hundred yards or so in front of the muzzles of our divisional 25-pounders.

At the time, I thought I was being kept there for a rest and check up. The doctors discovered that I had developed a pulse irregularity that gave the medical officer some concern. Just before I was to be released from medical care, the MO also noticed that my speech was slightly impaired. He examined my sore and swollen nose and found a considerable amount of congealed blood.

As a result, the MO was of the opinion that my immediate return to the Sniper Wing was not in the best interests for me or the army.

I then spent four or five days in an induced sleep, before making a full recovery and released to occupy another OP. This time it was a farmhouse with an excellent dry cellar on higher ground, about a couple of hundred yards or so west of the shell-damaged cottage I'd recently vacated. While I'd been recuperating in the Casualty Clearing Station, our battalion signallers had carried out a night operation to extend signal lines to the farmhouse. After returning to our forward positions each evening, headquarter stretcher-bearers were available to change dressings on my chest.

The effects of months living as a sniper had begun to take their toll on me. The on-going vigilance required during the daily routine of a sniper in 8th Brigade left little or no time for complacency. I needed to be constantly more than just alert when close to enemy lines. It inevitably made me tense and edgy. I realised I was exercising more caution than I'd done in the past and was also showing mild symptoms of a lack in concentration.

Although my facial injuries required an X-ray, it would be about two months before I could be taken to the 108 British General Hospital near Brussels. I had to wait until 3rd Division was enjoying a rare couple of days out of the line, which coincided with our move up into the spring offensive and crossing the German border.

We spent one unusual night near the small Dutch town of Tilburg on our way back into action. Tilburg at the time was directly beneath the flight paths of the enemy's V1 rockets, the ones destined for London and Antwerp. As the crow flies, it wasn't that far away from where the enemy was making mass launchings of the deadly V missiles. Many of them failed to reach their intended destinations and a few malfunctioned, subsequently detonating around the Tilburg area.

It seemed the Germans were intent on using all their surplus rockets in a hurry, fearing their launch sites would soon be over-run. The area around Tilburg was appropriately nicknamed "Doodle Bug Alley". Not surprisingly, Dutch civilians around the Tilburg district who were aware of our division's immediate destination, were overjoyed to hear the washing would be soon hanging out along the not too far away Siegfried Line.

It was around this time that I had the now long overdue X-ray, which revealed that part of the septum needed to be removed. This, together with my acute hearing difficulties, added to my concern for the state of my overall health.

Now, back in civvies, the damage to my hearing and other minor problems weren't helping me to get through lectures and other aspects of the tightly scheduled training program I'd undertaken. There were times when I'd felt a bit down and a little sorry for myself. I had lost eighty percent of my hearing and wasted five years of my life in the army, years I'd most likely have spent improving my elementary education in order to complete my then planned future in engineering.

Thankfully, during my time at the government training centre, I was very ably supported by other recently de-mobbed servicemen in my class. Some of these fellows had suffered horrific war injuries, particularly two or three ex-RAF aircrew, and a couple of chaps from tank regiments who'd been victims of blazing fuel.

A couple of these young men were in my class, each of them was partly devoid of their original facial features and carried the scars of large skin grafts. Even for a hardened ex-infantryman like me it took a little while to get used to their sorrowful war afflicted appearances. But I ended up being very grateful for the help they gave me, knowing that without their assistance, especially that of a Brummie named Richardson, I would most probably have failed the course.

My troubles certainly paled into insignificance alongside theirs. In fact, just a few weeks at the college witnessing the way they'd ignored their war injuries, life suddenly became a lot sweeter for me. If I had been harbouring any feelings of self-pity, they were quickly forgotten. In the company of these unfortunate men I realised I'd returned from the war one of the luckier ones.

This change in attitude was what I'd benefited most at the training centre, not the certificate of proficiency I received on completing the course. However, one thing did keep troubling me. I'd woken up to the fact that I'd returned to a life in Civvy Street without the happy-go-lucky disposition that I took into the army. That must have deserted me somewhere along the way during the years following my enlistment.

This became more noticeable when attending dances and other social functions, particularly those involving the opposite sex. There were times when I was sure I'd have felt more at ease when laying out in No Man's Land. Partying and get-togethers seemed like a new world to me; for most of the last five years, all my teen years, I'd lived in a vacuum in that regard.

Even those late evening sessions at the Gospel Oak seemed to have changed somewhat since my return to civvies; they were no longer singing those patriotic tearjerkers, the ones they often used to sing at night with a backing of gun fire during the early war years. Gone were those glory days of we're going to hang out the washing and the like. They obviously no longer wished to be reminded about the times we'd laughed and joked and sometimes cried, on our way to achieving that impossible dream. It seemed the public didn't want any reminder of all the misery and suffering as well as the terrible loss of so many innocent young lives, lives that were the ultimate cost of making that washing day possible.

By June, 1948, I was living in Australia, initially working as an electrician during the early stages of the Warragamba Dam project in New South Wales, about forty miles west of Sydney. Only three days before I'd left the *SS Ormonde* in Melbourne with no more than a few shillings and the clothes I stood in were all my worldly possessions.

This lack of funds forced me into saving some cash before I could take a more intimate look around the Sydney area, but it wasn't hard: I thoroughly enjoyed my new life at Warragamba, where we had barrack-style accommodation and many of my workmates were ex-servicemen. Most weekends were spent hiking to get away from the bustling activity surrounding the dam site, this to fish and swim along the banks of the Nepean River, most of that time from a base camp we'd set up in a cave beneath over hanging rocks at the mouth of Erskine Creek.

By January the following year, I'd begun to get itchy feet again and was able to reminisce when travelling in an old chartered ex-military DC3 while crossing the Owen Stanley Mountain Range en-route to Rabaul in New Britain. Rabaul at that time was still showing the scars of four years of Japanese occupation and Allied bombing, its beautiful natural harbour littered with wrecks of many Japanese warships and freighters.

Exploring these wrecks, along with an endless number of caves, tunnels and other now-obsolete Japanese shore installations, soon became the focus of a lot of my weekend leisure-time, while I found the various types of fishing available near Rabaul and adjacent islands were well worth travelling half-way around the world for.

After just five or six months working in Rabaul, my electrical qualifications helped me secure a second engineer's position on a passenger-freighter, and I enjoyed the next couple of years cruising around the South Pacific.

Early in 1950, I met my future wife, Bunty, when holidaying at North Stradbroke Island's Cylinder Beach, which, since shortly after arriving in Australia, had become my preferred home away from home and this later prompted me to sever the happy association I'd had with a life at sea.

Not long after the second of our three children had arrived, I was able to successfully complete a university course. This particular course had been abridged to be completed after eighteen-months' full-time study and was arranged and generously financed by my employer who wanted a surveyor with a qualified electrical background. This enabled me to spend the remaining thirty-odd years of my working life as a surveyor, mainly within the electricity supply industry.

Most of that time was spent in the survey and design associated with the construction of power and substations along with the early stages of South East Queensland's high voltage transmission grid. Here, I again found myself traversing beautiful and often sparsely occupied countryside, a telescope once again my companion, but this time amidst friendlier surroundings and motives that were a lot less sinister.

During my years as a surveyor, I'd been offered several opportunities of promotion to take up a position in the company's survey-design and development department, but my hearing problem ruled out any permanent office appointment and was in fact one of the main reasons for my transition into surveying. Apart from that, I felt the time I'd spent in the role of a sniper as an eighteen-year-old must have had more than a little influence on my future. This I realised during my early years as a surveyor, where I was again operating in quiet and sometimes very remote areas, independently having to make decisions of consequence and once again using the landscape to the best of my advantage.

To me, this didn't seem like a regular occupation at all. I felt it was a projection of a life that, by chance, had been nurtured for me as a young soldier when discreetly sounding out pockets of Normandy's sometimes mysterious bocage, while on other occasions ominously negotiating hedgerows, woodlands and sunken lanes.

Those hideous bygone days, the days of the deadly Nebelwerfer bombings that had so often preceded much blood and burials were non-existent in my new role of course, and the cuisine a lot more palatable and regular, thank goodness. But I must admit there'd been a few odd occasions that I'd spent tramping Queensland's beautiful rural areas where, conjured up in the back of my mind, I was once again dedicated to and carrying out assignments in a mannerism that I'd perceived during those glory days of 8th Infantry Brigade.

Unlike so many of his Royal Air Force colleagues and a few of his old school mates who never made it back to Birmingham's southern suburbs, my elder brother John survived the war. He'd got his wish, being called up by the RAF within days of reaching his eighteenth birthday, becoming a pilot at the age of nineteen. After his return to the UK from America, where he'd received his wings at Florida's Pensacola, courtesy of the US Navy, John was quickly sent out to Africa.

Then, after immigrating to Australia in 1947, he enjoyed a year or so managing a plantation on the north coast of New Britain. He, too, was able to sail the South Pacific after becoming the Mate, and later getting back into all the excitement as skipper of the 130-foot ketch *Raluana*, helping to successfully bring the damaged vessel several hundred miles to safety through a severe cyclone, this while engaged in island trading out of Rabaul.

One of the saddest stories was that of my old classmate, Jimmy Jackson, the lad who didn't want to be a footslogger. He'd waited patiently until the Royal Navy eventually got around to sending for him soon after he'd reached the tender age of sixteen. Jimmy must have been elated following his call-up and at last given the chance to don the blue uniform. But, for Jimmy, his joy would have been short-lived. He was killed within just a few months of his enlistment. I never ever got to see Jim in the uniform he'd waited so long to get. The last time I saw him was during the Blitz, when we'd met in Fred's Cafe in Acock's Green Village while on my first forty-eight-hour leave pass in 1940.

Jimmy had been a lovely lad. I can imagine there would have been a great many tears spilled on his passing. He was much too young, intelligent and nice to go so soon, even in wartime.

One of the big achievers was Joe Bridgwater, that mate of mine who, as a civilian, was unfortunate enough to lose an eye while extinguishing German incendiary bombs, during the worst days of the Blitz, mid November, 1940. Then, while still a teenager, and despite having minute pieces of shrapnel still embedded in his head and chest, he somehow managed to wangle his way into the army, enlisting in January, 1942, and was soon to become a corporal in the Royal Engineers.

One of Joe's last assignments was during April, 1945, only days before the war in Europe ended, when he led a team of sappers in the removal of an enemy 1500lb demolition charge from the abutments of the damaged Arnhem Bridge. Knowing the strife he'd encountered in 1940, one could only admire his courage in undertaking assignments of that kind.

Sergeant Joe Bridgwater left the army early in 1947, and he too migrated to Australia just a few months later, spending some time in New Guinea as a building contractor and later as a junior officer aboard a freighter sailing the South Pacific.

Joe finally settled in Queensland, where he built himself a Tudor-style home near the water's edge at Ormiston on Moreton Bay, his new lifestyle quite a contrast to that of his very modest boyhood days spent at Tenby Road in suburban Brummagem.

My feelings were that when taking into account his disability and its traumatic effects prior to his enlistment, few could claim to have made a bolder effort than Joe in helping to get the washing out on the Siegfried Line. For all his travelling, he'd always remained a faithful supporter of the "Blues", the Birmingham City Football Club.

In 1976, thirty-five years after the death of my army mate Eddie Atkinson, I made my first visit back to the United Kingdom, this after an absence of twenty-eight years.

For the first couple of months, my wife and I drove around the UK visiting places as far apart as Aberdeen and Land's End, spending a week or so at Torquay, where we stayed at a lovely hotel that was hosted by a former schoolmate who'd also been an old army colleague. Bernard "Bunny" Bevington, from Acock's Green, had landed by glider at Arnhem with my old battalion, the 2nd South Staffordshires, and before being taken prisoner had suffered severe head wounds.

His very caring wife, Jo, quietly asked me to try to avoid discussing the war with him, as any excitement brought on in that regard could have serious consequences. Bunny obviously still had the legacy of September 1944 hanging over him.

We'd arrived at Torquay in the middle of the holiday season only to find the hotel booked out and, since no pre-booking had been made and the only accommodation available was the bridal suite, we had our second honeymoon.

Before farewelling the Bevingtons, who, even though catering for at least a hundred other holiday guests, had arranged for my wife and I to be wined and dined like royalty for at least ten days, then on our departure refused to accept a penny towards an account that must have been enormous. We decided to drive over to the Gosport cemetery for a much-delayed visit to Eddie Atkinson's grave.

After parking near the cemetery gates, I expected to walk directly to it, believing it to be about forty yards or so from the main entrance. This was not the case, and half-an-hour of frustration later I still hadn't been able to find it. The unexpected delay prompted my wife Bunty to suggest that, because it was a long time ago, maybe I'd been imagining the military funeral and that perhaps it had never actually taken place.

'You've got to remember,' she told me, 'you were only a boy when you say your friend was killed, and, because of all the happenings around that time of the Blitz, you could have easily imagined all this.'

We were standing at the spot where I'd estimated the military funeral had taken place. I was very upset and beginning to wonder if it was conceivable there was some merit in what my wife had said, and wondering if maybe the war had had a bigger effect on me than I'd been made aware. We called off the search because we had limited time, deciding we should head off in the direction of Bulford to take another quick look at Carter Barracks for old time's sake, with time for my wife to take a look at Stonehenge, which was only a couple of miles from the place where I'd first donned the red beret.

While walking back through the cemetery, I noticed a chap who appeared to be taking down notes and looked as if he might help us with our problem, and, shortly after telling him my story about a mate being buried here directly between the graves of German airmen in February, 1941, he was able to tell us that back in the late 1940s any remaining graves of service personnel had been relocated to a plot in a far corner of the cemetery. The mystery surrounding Eddie's grave was solved.

And so, it wasn't long before my wife and I were standing at Eddie Atkinson's final resting place, paying our respects to my old army mate.

*

And suppose we'd never had that war?

I'm pretty sure that, over the years, I'd have eventually been able to associate myself with a customary spot on the bleachers at Villa Park. Then, after biding my time for a few more years I'd have probably found myself becoming acquainted with a "regular's seat" in a quiet corner of the public bar at our local, the Gospel Oak, unconcerned about an ever-increasing waistline while secretly harbouring a faint passion to be participating in a game of dominoes or cribbage, no doubt.

My keen interest in engineering during early 1940 had been such that I'd have probably gone on to become at the least, a very skilled machine toolmaker, most likely specialising in the field of high-grade jig and fixture design. And, who knows, may well have succeeded Harry Sharp or one of his successors, becoming toolroom foreman at Webley and Scott, happy to be painstakingly endeavouring to hold down that prestigious collar and tie job for the rest of my working days.

*

So, there you are. Of all the untold millions who'd suffered that horrible war, I'd have to say, in many ways it did one person a bit of good.

Sincerely,
Joe Lake

www.ingramcontent.com/pod-product-compliance
Lightning Source LLC
Chambersburg PA
CBHW072132160426
43197CB00012B/2079